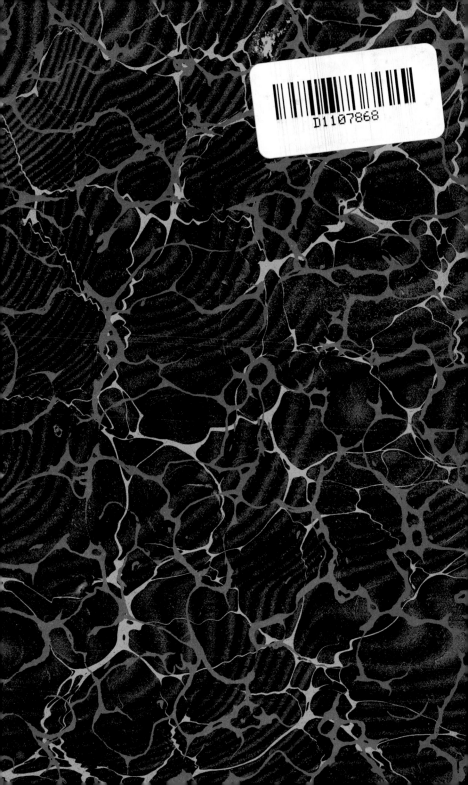

Ex-Libris

Ro Mar

The

R. D. Wardens

Hillcrest Edition

THE WRITINGS OF
MARK TWAIN
VOLUME XXII

This is the authorized
Uniform Edition of all
my books.
                Mark Twain

1899

From a photograph taken in 1899.
By H. W. Barnett, London.

HOW TO TELL A STORY

AND

OTHER ESSAYS

BY

MARK TWAIN
(Samuel L. Clemens)

NEW YORK AND LONDON
HARPER & BROTHERS PUBLISHERS

ILLUSTRATIONS

PHOTOGRAVURE

CONTENTS

Acknowledgment is hereby made to Harper & Brothers, The Century Company, The Cosmopolitan, and S. S. McClure & Co., for courtesy shown in allowing the reprint in this volume of a number of their articles.

HOW TO TELL A STORY

AND

OTHER ESSAYS

but no art is necessary in telling the comic and the witty story; anybody can do it. The art of telling a humorous story — understand, I mean by word of mouth, not print — was created in America, and has remained at home.

The humorous story is told gravely; the teller does his best to conceal the fact that he even dimly suspects that there is anything funny about it; but the teller of the comic story tells you beforehand that it is one of the funniest things he has ever heard, then tells it with eager delight, and is the first person to laugh when he gets through. And sometimes, if he has had good success, he is so glad and happy that he will repeat the " nub " of it and glance around from face to face, collecting applause, and then repeat it again. It is a pathetic thing to see.

Very often, of course, the rambling and disjointed humorous story finishes with a nub, point, snapper, or whatever you like to call it. Then the listener must be alert, for in many cases the teller will divert attention from that nub by dropping it in a carefully casual and indifferent way, with the pretence that he does not know it is a nub.

Artemus Ward used that trick a good deal; then when the belated audience presently caught the joke he would look up with innocent surprise, as if wondering what they had found to laugh at. Dan Setchell used it before him, Nye and Riley and others use it to-day.

But the teller of the comic story does not slur the nub; he shouts it at you — every time. And when he prints it, in England, France, Germany, and Italy, he italicizes it, puts some whooping exclamation-points after it, and sometimes explains it in a parenthesis. All of which is very depressing, and makes one want to renounce joking and lead a better life.

Let me set down an instance of the comic method, using an anecdote which has been popular all over the world for twelve or fifteen hundred years. The teller tells it in this way:

THE WOUNDED SOLDIER.

In the course of a certain battle a soldier whose leg had been shot off appealed to another soldier who was hurrying by to carry him to the rear, informing him at the same time of the loss which he had sustained; whereupon the generous son of Mars, shouldering the unfortunate, proceeded to carry out his desire. The bullets and cannon-balls were flying in all directions, and presently one of the latter took the wounded man's head off — without, however, his deliverer being aware of it. In no long time he was hailed by an officer, who said:

" Where are you going with that carcass?"

" To the rear, sir — he's lost his leg!"

" His leg, forsooth?" responded the astonished officer; " you mean his head, you booby."

Whereupon the soldier dispossessed himself of his

apparently absent-minded pause add an incongru-
ous remark in a soliloquizing way; and that was
the remark intended to explode the mine — and
it did.

For instance, he would say eagerly, excitedly, " I
once knew a man in New Zealand who hadn't a
tooth in his head "— here his animation would die
out; a silent, reflective pause would follow, then he
would say dreamily, and as if to himself, " and yet
that man could beat a drum better than any man I
ever saw."

The pause is an exceedingly important feature in
any kind of story, and a frequently recurring feature,
too. It is a dainty thing, and delicate, and also uncertain and treacherous; for it must be exactly the
right length — no more and no less — or it fails of
its purpose and makes trouble. If the pause is too
short the impressive point is passed, and the audience have had time to divine that a surprise is
intended — and then you can't surprise them, of
course.

On the platform I used to tell a negro ghost story
that had a pause in front of the snapper on the end,
and that pause was the most important thing in the
whole story. If I got it the right length precisely,
I could spring the finishing ejaculation with effect
enough to make some impressible girl deliver a
startled little yelp and jump out of her seat — and
that was what I was after. This story was called
" The Golden Arm," and was told in this fashion.

You can practise with it yourself — and mind you look out for the pause and get it right.

THE GOLDEN ARM.

Once 'pon a time dey wuz a monsus mean man, en he live 'way out in de prairie all 'lone by hisself, 'cep'n he had a wife. En bimeby she died, en he tuck en toted her way out dah in de prairie en buried her. Well, she had a golden arm — all solid gold, fum de shoulder down. He wuz pow'ful mean — pow'ful; en dat night he couldn't sleep, caze he want dat golden arm so bad.

When it come midnight he couldn't stan' it no mo'; so he git up, he did, en tuck his lantern en shoved out thoo de storm en dug her up en got de golden arm; en he bent his head down 'gin de win', en plowed en plowed en plowed thoo de snow. Den all on a sudden he stop (make a considerable pause here, and look startled, and take a listening attitude) en say: "My *lan*', what's dat!"

En he listen — en listen — en de win' say (set your teeth together and imitate the wailing and wheezing singsong of the wind), "Bzzz-z-zzz "— en den, way back yonder whah de grave is, he hear a *voice !* — he hear a voice all mix' up in de win' — can't hardly tell 'em 'part — "Bzzz-zzz — W-h-o — g-o-t — m-y — g-o-l-d-e-n *arm?* — zzz — zzz — W-h-o g-o-t m-y g-o-l-d-e-n *arm ?*" (You must begin to shiver violently now.)

En he begin to shiver en shake, en say, "Oh,

2 E

my! *Oh*, my lan'!'' en de win' blow de lantern out, en de snow en sleet blow in his face en mos' choke him, en he start a-plowin' knee-deep towards home mos' dead, he so sk'yerd — en pooty soon he hear de voice agin, en (pause) it 'us comin' *after* him! '' Bzzz — zzz — zzz — W-h-o — g-o-t — m-y — g-o-l-d-e-n — *arm?*''

When he git to de pasture he hear it agin — closter now, en a-*comin'!* — a-comin' back dah in de dark en de storm — (repeat the wind and the voice). When he git to de house he rush up-stairs en jump in de bed en kiver up, head and years, en lay dah shiverin' en shakin' — en den way out dah he hear it *agin!* — en a-*comin'!* En bimeby he hear (pause — awed, listening attitude) — pat — pat — pat —*hit's a-comin' up-stairs!* Den he hear de latch, en he *know* it's in de room!

Den pooty soon he know it's a-*stannin'* by de bed! (Pause.) Den — he know it's a-*bendin' down over him* — en he cain't skasely git his breath! Den — den — he seem to feel someth'n *c-o-l-d*, right down 'most agin his head! (Pause.)

Den de voice say, *right at his year* — '' W-h-o — g-o-t — m-y — g-o-l-d-e-n *arm?*'' (You must wail it out very plaintively and accusingly; then you stare steadily and impressively into the face of the farthest-gone auditor — a girl, preferably — and let that awe-inspiring pause begin to build itself in the deep hush. When it has reached exactly the right length, jump suddenly at that girl and yell, "*You've* got it!"

If you've got the *pause* right, she'll fetch a dear little yelp and spring right out of her shoes. But you *must* get the pause right; and you will find it the most troublesome and aggravating and uncertain thing you ever undertook.)

IN DEFENCE OF HARRIET SHELLEY

I

I HAVE committed sins, of course; but I have not committed enough of them to entitle me to the punishment of reduction to the bread and water of ordinary literature during six years when I might have been living on the fat diet spread for the righteous in Professor Dowden's *Life of Shelley*, if I had been justly dealt with.

During these six years I have been living a life of peaceful ignorance. I was not aware that Shelley's first wife was unfaithful to him, and that that was why he deserted her and wiped the stain from his sensitive honor by entering into soiled relations with Godwin's young daughter. This was all new to me when I heard it lately, and was told that the proofs of it were in this book, and that this book's verdict is accepted in the girls' colleges of America and its view taught in their literary classes.

In each of these six years multitudes of young people in our country have arrived at the Shelley-reading age. Are these six multitudes unacquainted with this life of Shelley? Perhaps they are; indeed,

one may feel pretty sure that the great bulk of them
are.   To these, then, I address myself, in the hope
that some account of this romantic historical fable
and the fabulist's manner of constructing and adorn-
ing it may interest them.

First, as to its literary style. Our negroes in
America have several ways of entertaining themselves which are not found among the whites any-
where. Among these inventions of theirs is one
which is particularly popular with them. It is a
competition in elegant deportment. They hire a
hall and bank the spectators' seats in rising tiers
along the two sides, leaving all the middle stretch of
the floor free. A cake is provided as a prize for
the winner in the competition, and a bench of experts in deportment is appointed to award it. Sometimes there are as many as fifty contestants, male
and female, and five hundred spectators. One at a
time the contestants enter, clothed regardless of expense in what each considers the perfection of style
and taste, and walk down the vacant central space
and back again with that multitude of critical eyes
on them. All that the competitor knows of fine airs
and graces he throws into his carriage, all that he
knows of seductive expression he throws into his
countenance. He may use all the helps he can
devise: watch-chain to twirl with his fingers, cane
to do graceful things with, snowy handkerchief to
flourish and get artful effects out of, shiny new
stovepipe hat to assist in his courtly bows; and the

2*.*.

colored lady may have a fan to work up *her* effects
with, and smile over and blush behind, and she
may add other helps, according to her judgment.
When the review by individual detail is over, a grand
review of all the contestants in procession follows,
with all the airs and graces and all the bowings and
smirkings on exhibition at once, and this enables
the bench of experts to make the necessary com-
parisons and arrive at a verdict. The successful
competitor gets the prize which I have before mentioned, and an abundance of applause and envy
along with it. The negroes have a name for this
grave deportment-tournament; a name taken from
the prize contended for. They call it a Cake-
Walk.

This Shelley biography is a literary cake-walk.
The ordinary forms of speech are absent from it.
All the pages, all the paragraphs, walk by sedately,
elegantly, not to say mincingly, in their Sunday-
best, shiny and sleek, perfumed, and with *bouton-
nieres* in their button-holes; it is rare to find even a
chance sentence that has forgotten to dress. If the
book wishes to tell us that Mary Godwin, child of
sixteen, had known afflictions, the fact saunters
forth in this nobby outfit: " Mary was herself not
unlearned in the lore of pain " — meaning by that
that she had not always traveled on asphalt; or, as
some authorities would frame it, that she had " been
there herself," a form which, while preferable to the
book's form, is still not to be recommended. If the

book wishes to tell us that Harriet Shelley hired a wet-nurse, that commonplace fact gets turned into a dancing-master, who does his professional bow before us in pumps and knee-breeches, with his fiddle under one arm and his crush-hat under the other, thus: " The beauty of Harriet's motherly relation to her babe was marred in Shelley's eyes by the introduction into his house of a hireling nurse to whom was delegated the mother's tenderest office."

This is perhaps the strangest book that has seen the light since Frankenstein. Indeed, it is a Frankenstein itself; a Frankenstein with the original infirmity supplemented by a new one; a Frankenstein with the reasoning faculty wanting. Yet it believes it can reason, and is always trying. It is not content to leave a mountain of fact standing in the clear sunshine, where the simplest reader can perceive its form, its details, and its relation to the rest of the landscape, but thinks it must help him examine it and understand it; so its drifting mind settles upon it with that intent, but always with one and the same result: there is a change of temperature and the mountain is hid in a fog. Every time it sets up a premise and starts to reason from it, there is a surprise in store for the reader. It is strangely near-sighted, cross-eyed, and purblind. Sometimes when a mastodon walks across the field of its vision it takes it for a rat; at other times it does not see it at all.

B*₊*₊

The materials of this biographical fable are facts, rumors, and poetry. They are connected together and harmonized by the help of suggestion, conjecture, innuendo, perversion, and semi-suppression.

The fable has a distinct object in view, but this object is not acknowledged in set words. Percy Bysshe Shelley has done something which in the case of other men is called a grave crime; it must be shown that in his case it is not that, because he does not think as other men do about these things.

Ought not that to be enough, if the fabulist is serious? Having proved that a crime is not a crime, was it worth while to go on and fasten the responsibility of a crime which was not a crime upon somebody else? What is the use of hunting down and holding to bitter account people who are responsible for other people's innocent acts?

Still, the fabulist thinks it a good idea to do that. In his view Shelley's first wife, Harriet, free of all offense as far as we have historical facts for guidance, must be held unforgivably responsible for her husband's innocent act in deserting her and taking up with another woman.

Any one will suspect that this task has its difficulties. Any one will divine that nice work is necessary here, cautious work, wily work, and that there is entertainment to be had in watching the magician do it. There is indeed entertainment in watching him. He arranges his facts, his rumors, and his poems on his table in full view of the house, and shows you

that everything is there — no deception, everything
fair and above board.   And this is apparently true,
yet there is a defect, for some of his best stock is
hid in an appendix-basket behind the door, and you
do not come upon it until the exhibition is over and
the enchantment of your mind accomplished — as
the magician thinks.

There is an insistent atmosphere of candor and
fairness about this book which is engaging at first,
then a little burdensome, then a trifle fatiguing, then
progressively suspicious, annoying, irritating, and
oppressive.   It takes one some little time to find out
that phrases which seem intended to guide the reader
aright are there to mislead him; that phrases which
seem intended to throw light are there to throw
darkness; that phrases which seem intended to
interpret a fact are there to misinterpret it; that
phrases which seem intended to forestall prejudice
are there to create it; that phrases which seem anti-
dotes are poisons in disguise.   The naked facts
arrayed in the book establish Shelley's guilt in that
one episode which disfigures his otherwise super-
latively lofty and beautiful life; but the historian's
careful and methodical misinterpretation of them
transfers the responsibility to the wife's shoulders —
as he persuades himself.   The few meagre facts of
Harriet Shelley's life, as furnished by the book,
acquit her of offense; but by calling in the forbidden helps of rumor, gossip, conjecture, insinua-
tion, and innuendo he destroys her character and

Shelley was nineteen. He was not a youth, but a man. He had never had any youth. He was an erratic and fantastic child during eighteen years, then he stepped into manhood, as one steps over a door-sill. He was curiously mature at nineteen in his ability to do independent thinking on the deep questions of life and to arrive at sharply definite decisions regarding them, and stick to them — stick to them and stand by them at cost of bread, friend-ships, esteem, respect, and approbation.

For the sake of his opinions he was willing to sacrifice all these valuable things, and did sacrifice them; and went on doing it, too, when he could at any moment have made himself rich and supplied himself with friends and esteem by compromising with his father, at the moderate expense of throwing overboard one or two indifferent details of his cargo of principles.

He and Harriet eloped to Scotland and got mar-ried. They took lodgings in Edinburgh of a sort answerable to their purse, which was about empty, and there their life was a happy one and grew daily more so. They had only themselves for company, but they needed no additions to it. They were as cozy and contented as birds in a nest. Harriet sang evenings or read aloud; also she studied and tried to improve her mind, her husband instructing her in Latin. She was very beautiful, she was modest, quiet, genuine, and, according to her husband's testimony, she had no fine lady airs or aspirations

about her.   In Matthew Arnold's judgment, she
was " a pleasing figure."

The pair remained five weeks in Edinburgh, and
then took lodgings in York, where Shelley's college
mate, Hogg, lived.   Shelley presently ran down to
London, and Hogg took this opportunity to make
love to the young wife.   She repulsed him, and reported the fact to her husband when he got back.
It seems a pity that Shelley did not copy this credit-
able conduct of hers some time or other when under
temptation, so that we might have seen the author
of his biography hang the miracle in the skies and
squirt rainbows at it.

At the end of the first year of marriage — the
most trying year for any young couple, for then the
mutual failings are coming one by one to light, and
the necessary adjustments are being made in pain
and tribulation — Shelley was able to recognize that
his marriage venture had been a safe one.   As we
have seen, his love for his wife had begun in a
rather shallow way and with not much force, but
now it was become deep and strong, which entitles
his wife to a broad credit mark, one may admit.
He addresses a long and loving poem to her, in
which both passion and worship appear:

Exhibit A

" O thou
Whose dear love gleamed upon the gloomy path
Which this lone spirit travelled,

.   .   .   .

. . . wilt thou not turn

Exhibit D

"EVENING.   TO HARRIET

" O thou bright Sun !   Beneath the dark blue line
Of western distance that sublime descendest,
And, gleaming lovelier as thy beams decline,
Thy million hues to every vapor lendest,
And over cobweb, lawn, and grove, and stream
Sheddest the liquid magic of thy light,
Till calm Earth, with the parting splendor bright,
Shows like the vision of a beauteous dream;
What gazer now with astronomic eye
Could coldly count the spots within thy sphere ?
Such were thy lover, Harriet, could he fly
The thoughts of all that makes his passion dear,
And turning senseless from thy warm caress
Pick flaws in our close-woven happiness."

I cannot find the " rift "; still it may be there.
What the poem *seems* to say is, that a person would
be coldly ungrateful who could consent to count and
consider little spots and flaws in such a warm, great,
satisfying sun as Harriet is.   It is a " little rift
which had seemed to be healed, *or* never to have
gaped at all."   That is, " one *detects* " a little rift
which perhaps had never existed.   How does one
do that ?   How does one see the invisible?   It is the
fabulist's secret; he knows how to detect what does
not exist, he knows how to see what is not seeable;
it is his gift, and he works it many a time to poor
dead Harriet Shelley's deep damage.

" As yet, however, if there was a speck upon
Shelley's happiness it was no more than a speck "
—meaning the one which one detects where " it

may never have gaped at all '' — '' nor had Harriet cause for discontent.''

Shelley's Latin instructions to his wife had ceased. '' From a teacher he had now become a pupil.'' Mrs. Boinville and her young married daughter Cornelia were teaching him Italian poetry; a fact which warns one to receive with some caution that other statement that Harriet had no '' cause for discontent.''

Shelley had stopped instructing Harriet in Latin, as before mentioned. The biographer thinks that the busy life in London some time back, and the intrusion of the baby, account for this. These were hindrances, but were there no others? He is always overlooking a detail here and there that might be valuable in helping us understand a situation. For instance, when a man has been hard at work at the Italian poets with a pretty woman, hour after hour, and responding like a tremulous instrument to every breath of passion or of sentiment in the meantime, that man is dog-tired when he gets home, and he *can't* teach his wife Latin; it would be unreasonable to expect it.

Up to this time we have submitted to having Mrs. Boinville pushed upon us as ostensibly concerned in these Italian lessons, but the biographer drops her now, of his own accord. Cornelia '' perhaps '' is sole teacher. Hogg says she was a prey to a kind of sweet melancholy, arising from causes purely imaginary; she required consolation, and found it

3E

in Petrarch. He also says, " Bysshe entered at once fully into her views and caught the soft infection, breathing the tenderest and sweetest melancholy, as every true poet ought."

Then the author of the book interlards a most stately and fine compliment to Cornelia, furnished by a man of approved judgment who knew her well " in later years." It is a very good compliment indeed, and she no doubt deserved it in her " later years," when she had for generations ceased to be sentimental and lackadaisical, and was no longer engaged in enchanting young husbands and sowing sorrow for young wives. But why is that compliment to that old gentlewoman intruded there? Is it to make the reader believe she was well-chosen and safe society for a young, sentimental husband? The biographer's device was not well planned. That old person was not present — it was her other self that was there, her young, sentimental, melancholy, warm-blooded self, in those early sweet times before antiquity had cooled her off and mossed her back.

" In choosing for friends such women as Mrs. Newton, Mrs. Boinville, and Cornelia Turner, Shelley gave good proof of his insight and discrimination." That is the fabulist's opinion — Harriet Shelley's is not reported.

Early in August, Shelley was in London trying to raise money. In September he wrote the poem to the baby, already quoted from. In the first week of October Shelley and family went to Warwick,

then to Edinburgh, arriving there about the middle
of the month.

"Harriet was happy." Why? The author furnishes a reason, but hides from us whether it is
history or conjecture; it is because "*the babe had
borne the journey well.*" It has all the aspect of one
of his artful devices — flung in in his favorite casual
way — the way he has when he wants to draw one's
attention away from an obvious thing and amuse it
with some trifle that is less obvious but more useful
— in a history like this. The obvious thing is, that
Harriet was happy because there was much territory
between her husband and Cornelia Turner now; and
because the perilous Italian lessons were taking a
rest; and because, if there chanced to be any re-
spondings like a tremulous instrument to every
breath of passion or of sentiment in stock in these
days, she might hope to get a share of them herself;
and because, with her husband liberated, now, from
the fetid fascinations of that sentimental retreat so
pitilessly described by Hogg, who also dubbed it
"Shelley's paradise" later, she might hope to persuade him to stay away from it permanently; and
because she might also hope that his brain would
cool, now, and his heart become healthy, and both
brain and heart consider the situation and resolve
that it would be a right and manly thing to stand by
this girl-wife and her child and see that they were
honorably dealt with, and cherished and protected
and loved by the man that had promised these

things, and so be made happy and kept so. And because, also — may we conjecture this? — we may hope for the privilege of taking up our cozy Latin lessons again, that used to be so pleasant, and brought us so near together — so near, indeed, that often our heads touched, just as heads do over Italian lessons; and our hands met in casual and unintentional, but still most delicious and thrilling little contacts and momentary clasps, just as they inevitably do over Italian lessons. Suppose one should say to any young wife: " I find that your husband is poring over the Italian poets and being instructed in the beautiful Italian language by the lovely Cornelia Robinson " — would that cozy picture fail to rise before her mind? would its possibilities fail to suggest themselves to her? would there be a pang in her heart and a blush on her face? or, on the contrary, would the remark give her pleasure, make her joyous and gay? Why, one needs only to make the experiment — the result will not be uncertain.

However, we learn — by authority of deeply reasoned and searching conjecture — that the baby bore the journey well, and that that was why the young wife was happy. That accounts for two per cent. of the happiness, but it was not right to imply that it accounted for the other ninety-eight also.

Peacock, a scholar, poet, and friend of the Shelleys, was of their party when they went away. He used to laugh at the Boinville menagerie, and " was not a favorite." One of the Boinville group, writing to Hogg, said, " The Shelleys have made an addition to their party in the person of a cold scholar, who, I think, has neither taste nor feeling. This, Shelley will perceive sooner or later, for his warm nature craves sympathy." True, and Shelley will fight his way back there to get it — there will be no way to head him off.

Towards the end of November it was necessary for Shelley to pay a business visit to London, and he conceived the project of leaving Harriet and the baby in Edinburgh with Harriet's sister, Eliza Westbrook, a sensible, practical maiden lady about thirty years old, who had spent a great part of her time with the family since the marriage. She was an estimable woman, and Shelley had had reason to like her, and did like her; but along about this time his feeling towards her changed. Part of Shelley's plan, as he wrote Hogg, was to spend his London evenings with the Newtons — members of the Boinville Hysterical Society. But, alas, when he arrived early in December, that pleasant game was partially blocked, for Eliza and the family arrived *with* him. We are left destitute of conjectures at this point by the biographer, and it is my duty to supply one. I chance the conjecture that it was Eliza who interfered with that game. I think she tried to do what she could towards modifying the Boinville connection, in the interest of her young sister's peace and honor.

3*₊*₊

If it was she who blocked that game, she was not strong enough to block the next one. Before the month and year were out — no date given, let us call it Christmas — Shelley and family were nested in a furnished house in Windsor, "at no great distance from the Boinvilles" — these decoys still residing at Bracknell.

What we need, now, is a misleading conjecture. We get it with characteristic promptness and depravity:

"But Prince Athanase found not the aged Zonoras, the friend of his boyhood, in any wanderings to Windsor. Dr. Lind had died a year since, and with his death Windsor must have lost, for Shelley, its chief attraction."

Still, not to mention Shelley's wife, there was Bracknell, at any rate. While Bracknell remains, all solace is not lost. Shelley is represented by this biographer as doing a great many careless things, but to my mind this hiring a furnished house for three months in order to be with a man who has been dead a year, is the carelessest of them all. One feels for him — that is but natural, and does us honor besides — yet one is vexed, for all that. He could have written and asked about the aged Zonoras before taking the house. He may not have had the address, but that is nothing — any postman would know the aged Zonoras; a dead postman would remember a name like that.

And yet, why throw a rag like this to us ravening wolves? Is it seriously supposable that we will stop to chew it and let our prey escape? No, we are getting to expect this kind of device, and to give it merely a sniff for certainty's sake and then walk around it and leave it lying. Shelley was not after the aged Zonoras; he was pointed for Cornelia and the Italian lessons, for his warm nature was craving sympathy.

II

THE year 1813 is just ended now, and we step into 1814.

To recapitulate, how much of Cornelia's society has Shelley had, thus far? Portions of August and September, and four days of July. That is to say, he has had opportunity to enjoy it, more or less, during that brief period. Did he want some more of it? We must fall back upon history, and then go to conjecturing.

"In the early part of the year 1814, Shelley was a frequent visitor at Bracknell."

"Frequent" is a cautious word, in this author's mouth; the very cautiousness of it, the vagueness of it, provokes suspicion; it makes one suspect that this frequency was more frequent than the mere common everyday kinds of frequency which one is in the habit of averaging up with the unassuming term "frequent." I think so because they fixed up a bedroom for him in the Boinville house. One

c*.*.

doesn't need a bedroom if one is only going to run over now and then in a disconnected way to respond like a tremulous instrument to every breath of passion or of sentiment and rub up one's Italian poetry a little.

The young wife was not invited, perhaps. If she was, she most certainly did not come, or she would have straightened the room up; the most ignorant of us knows that a wife would not endure a room in the condition in which Hogg found this one when he occupied it one night. Shelley was away — why, nobody can divine. Clothes were scattered about, there were books on every side: "Wherever a book could be laid was an open book turned down on its face to keep its place." It seems plain that the wife was not invited. No, not that; I think she was invited, but said to herself that she could not bear to go there and see another young woman touching heads with her husband over an Italian book and making thrilling hand-contacts with him accidentally.

As remarked, he was a frequent visitor there, "where he found an easeful resting-place in the house of Mrs. Boinville — the white-haired Maimuna — and of her daughter, Mrs. Turner." The aged Zonoras was deceased, but the white-haired Maimuna was still on deck, as we see. "Three charming ladies entertained the mocker (Hogg) with cups of tea, late hours, Wieland's Agathon, sighs and smiles, and the celestial manna of refined sentiment."

" Such," says Hogg, " were the delights of Shelley's paradise in Bracknell."

The white-haired Maimuna presently writes to
Hogg:

" I will not have you despise home-spun pleasures. Shelley is
making a trial of them with us —"

A trial of them. It may be called that. It was
March 11, and he had been in the house a month.
She continues:

Shelley "likes them so well that he is resolved to leave off rambling —"

But he has *already* left it off. He has been there
a month.

" And begin a course of them himself."

But he has already begun it. He has been at it a
month. He likes it so well that he has forgotten all
about his wife, as a letter of his reveals.

" Seriously, I think his mind and body want rest."

Yet he has been resting both for a month, with
Italian, and tea, and manna of sentiment, and late
hours, and every restful thing a young husband
could need for the refreshment of weary limbs and a
sore conscience, and a nagging sense of shabbiness
and treachery.

" His journeys after what he has never found have racked his purse
and his tranquillity. He is resolved to take a little care of the former,
in pity to the latter, which I applaud, and shall second with all my
might."

But she does not say whether the young wife, a

" I am now but little inclined to contest this point. I certainly hate her with all my heart and soul. . . .

" It is a sight which awakens an inexpressible sensation of disgust and horror, to see her caress my poor little Ianthe, in whom I may hereafter find the consolation of sympathy. I sometimes feel faint with the fatigue of checking the overflowings of my unbounded abhorrence for this miserable wretch. But she is no more than a blind and loathsome worm, that cannot see to sting.

" I have begun to learn Italian again. . . . Cornelia assists me in this language. Did I not once tell you that I thought her cold and reserved? She is the reverse of this, as she is the reverse of everything bad. She inherits all the divinity of her mother. . . . I have sometimes forgotten that I am not an inmate of this delightful home — that a time will come which will cast me again into the boundless ocean of abhorred society.

" I have written nothing but one stanza, which has no meaning, and that I have only written in thought:

" Thy dewy looks sink in my breast;
    Thy gentle words stir poison there;
Thou hast disturbed the only rest
    That was the portion of despair.
Subdued to duty's hard control,
    I could have borne my wayward lot:
The chains that bind this ruined soul
    Had cankered then, but crushed it not.

" This is the vision of a delirious and distempered dream, which passes away at the cold clear light of morning. Its surpassing excellence and exquisite perfections have no more reality than the color of an autumnal sunset."

Then it did not refer to his wife. That is plain; otherwise he would have said so. It is well that he explained that it has no meaning, for if he had not done that, the previous soft references to Cornelia and the way he has come to feel about her now would make us think she was the person who had inspired it while teaching him how to read the warm and ruddy Italian poets during a month.

The biography observes that portions of this letter "read like the tired moaning of a wounded creature." Guesses at the nature of the wound are permissible; we will hazard one.

Read by the light of Shelley's previous history, his letter seems to be the cry of a tortured conscience. Until this time it was a conscience that had never felt a pang or known a smirch. It was the conscience of one who, until this time, had never done a dishonorable thing, or an ungenerous, or cruel, or treacherous thing, but was now doing all of these, and was keenly aware of it. Up to this time Shelley had been master of his nature, and it was a nature which was as beautiful and as nearly perfect as any merely human nature may be. But he was drunk now, with a debasing passion, and was not himself. There is nothing in his previous history that is in character with the Shelley of this letter. He had done boyish things, foolish things, even crazy things, but never a thing to be ashamed of. He had done things which one might laugh at, but the privilege of laughing was limited always to the thing itself; you could not laugh at the motive back of it — that was high, that was noble. His most fantastic and quixotic acts had a purpose back of them which made them fine, often great, and made the rising laugh seem profanation and quenched it; quenched it, and changed the impulse to homage.

the biographical prosecuting attorney has set himself
the task of proving upon her.

Does the biographer *call* himself the attorney for
the prosecution? No, only to himself, privately;
publicly he is the passionless, disinterested, impartial
judge on the bench. He holds up his judicial scales
before the world, that all may see; and it all tries
to look so fair that a blind person would sometimes
fail to see him slip the false weights in.

Shelley's happiness in his home had been wounded
and bruised almost to death, first, because Harriet
had persuaded him to set up a carriage. I cannot
discover that any evidence is offered that she asked
him to set up a carriage. Still, if she did, was it a
heavy offence? Was it unique? Other young wives
had committed it before, others have committed it
since. Shelley had dearly loved her in those London days; possibly he set up the carriage gladly to
please her; affectionate young husbands do such
things. When Shelley ran away with another girl,
by-and-by, this girl persuaded him to pour the price
of many carriages and many horses down the
bottomless well of her father's debts, but this impartial judge finds no fault with that. Once she
appeals to Shelley to raise money — necessarily by
borrowing, there was no other way — to pay her
father's debts with at a time when Shelley was in
danger of being arrested and imprisoned for his own
debts; yet the good judge finds no fault with her
even for this.

First and last, Shelley emptied into that rapacious mendicant's lap a sum which cost him — for he borrowed it at ruinous rates — from eighty to one hundred thousand dollars. But it was Mary Godwin's papa, the supplications were often sent through Mary, the good judge is Mary's strenuous friend, so Mary gets no censures. On the Continent *Mary rode in her private carriage*, built, as Shelley boasts, " by one of the best makers in Bond Street," yet the good judge makes not even a passing comment on this iniquity. Let us throw out Count No. 1 against Harriet Shelley as being far-fetched and frivolous.

Shelley's happiness in his home had been wounded and bruised almost to death, secondly, because Harriet's studies " had dwindled away to nothing, Bysshe had ceased to express any interest in them." At what time was this? It was when Harriet " had fully recovered from the fatigue of her first effort of maternity,. . . and was now in full force, vigor, and effect." Very well, the baby was born two days before the close of June. It took the mother a month to get back her full force, vigor, and effect; this brings us to July 27th and the deadly Cornelia. If a wife of eighteen is studying with her husband and he gets smitten with another woman, isn't he likely to lose interest in his wife's studies for *that* reason, and is not his wife's interest in her studies likely to languish for the *same* reason? Would not the mere sight of those books of hers sharpen the

4E

pain that is in her heart? This sudden breaking down of a mutual intellectual interest of two years' standing is coincident with Shelley's re-encounter with Cornelia; and we are allowed to gather from that time forth for nearly two months he did all his studying in that person's society. We feel at liberty to rule out Count No. 2 from the indictment against Harriet.

Shelley's happiness in his home had been wounded and bruised almost to death, thirdly, because Harriet's walks with Hogg commonly led to some fashionable bonnet-shop. I offer no palliation; I only ask why the dispassionate, impartial judge did not offer one himself — merely, I mean, to offset his leniency in a similar case or two where the girl who ran away with Harriet's husband was the shopper. There are several occasions where she interested herself with shopping — among them being walks which ended at the bonnet-shop — yet in none of these cases does she get a word of blame from the good judge, while in one of them he covers the deed with a justifying remark, she doing the shopping that time to find easement for her mind, her child having died.

Shelley's happiness in his home had been wounded and bruised almost to death, fourthly, by the intro-duction there of a wet-nurse. The wet-nurse was introduced at the time of the Edinburgh sojourn, immediately after Shelley had been enjoying the two months of study with Cornelia which broke up his wife's studies and destroyed his personal interest in them. Why, by this time, nothing that Shelley's wife could do would have been satisfactory to him, for he was in love with another woman, and was never going to be contented again until he got back to her. If he had been still in love with his wife it is not easily conceivable that he would care much who nursed the baby, provided the baby was well nursed. Harriet's jealousy was assuredly voicing itself now, Shelley's conscience was assuredly nagging him, pestering him, persecuting him. Shelley needed excuses for his altered attitude towards his wife; Providence pitied him and sent the wet-nurse. If Providence had sent him a cotton doughnut it would have answered just as well; all he wanted was something to find fault with.

Shelley's happiness in his home had been wounded and bruised almost to death, fifthly, because Harriet narrowly watched a surgical operation which was being performed upon her child, and, "to the astonishment of the operator," who was watching Harriet instead of attending to his operation, she betrayed "not the smallest sign of emotion." The author of this biography was not ashamed to set down that exultant slander. He was apparently not aware that it was a small business to bring into his court a witness whose name he does not know, and whose character and veracity there is none to vouch for, and allow him to strike this blow at the mother-heart of this friendless girl. The biographer

says, " We may not infer from this that Harriet did
not feel " — why put it in, then? —"but we learn
that those about her could believe her to be hard
and insensible." Who were those who were about
her? Her husband? He hated her now, because he
was in love elsewhere. Her sister? Of course that
is not charged. Peacock? Peacock does not testify.
The wet-nurse? She does not testify. If any others
were there we have no mention of them. " Those
about her " are reduced to one person — her husband. Who reports the circumstance? It is Hogg.
Perhaps he was there — we do not know. But if he
was, he still got his information at second-hand, as
it was the operator who noticed Harriet's lack of
emotion, not himself. Hogg is not given to saying
kind things when Harriet is his subject. He may
have said them the time that he tried to tempt her
to soil her honor, but after that he mentions her
usually with a sneer. " Among those who were
about her " was one witness well equipped to
silence all tongues, abolish all doubts, set our minds at
rest; one witness, not called, and not callable, whose
evidence, if we could but get it, would outweigh
the oaths of whole battalions of hostile Hoggs and
nameless surgeons — the baby. I wish we had the
baby's testimony; and yet if we had it it would not
do us any good — a furtive conjecture, a sly insinua-
tion, a pious " if " or two, would be smuggled in,
here and there, with a solemn air of judicial investi-
gation, and its positiveness would wilt into dubiety.

The biographer says of Harriet, " If words of tender affection and motherly pride proved the reality of love, then undoubtedly she loved her first-born child." That is, if mere empty words can prove it, it stands proved — and in this way, without committing himself, he gives the reader a chance to infer that there isn't any extant evidence but words, and that he doesn't take much stock in them. How seldom he shows his hand! He is always lurking behind a non-committal "if " or something of that kind; always gliding and dodging around, distributing colorless poison here and there and everywhere, but always leaving himself in a position to say that his language will be found innocuous if taken to pieces and examined. He clearly exhibits a steady and never-relaxing purpose to make Harriet the scapegoat for her husband's first great sin — but it is in the general view that this is revealed, not in the details. His insidious literature is like blue water; you know what it is that makes it blue, but you cannot produce and verify any detail of the cloud of microscopic dust in it that does it. Your adversary can dip up a glassful and show you that it is pure white and you cannot deny it; and he can dip the lake dry, glass by glass, and show that every glassful is white, and prove it to any one's eye — and yet that lake *was* blue and you can swear it. This book is blue — with slander in solution.

Let the reader examine, for example, the paragraph of comment which immediately follows the

4*.*.

letter containing Shelley's self-exposure which we have been considering. This is it. One should inspect the individual sentences as they go by, then pass them in procession and review the cake-walk as a whole:

" Shelley's happiness in his home, as is evident from this pathetic letter, had been fatally stricken; it is evident, also, that he knew where duty lay; he felt that his part was to take up his burden, silently and sorrowfully, and to bear it henceforth with the quietness of despair. But we can perceive that he scarcely possessed the strength and fortitude needful for success in such an attempt. And clearly Shelley himself was aware how perilous it was to accept that respite of blissful ease which he enjoyed in the Boinville household; for gentle voices and dewy looks and words of sympathy could not fail to remind him of an ideal of tranquillity or of joy which could never be his, and which he must henceforth sternly exclude from his imagination."

That paragraph commits the author in no way. Taken sentence by sentence it *asserts* nothing against anybody or in favor of anybody, pleads for nobody, accuses nobody. Taken detail by detail, it is as innocent as moonshine. And yet, taken as a whole, it is a design against the reader; its intent is to remove the feeling which the letter must leave with him if let alone, and put a different one in its place — to remove a feeling justified by the letter and substitute one not justified by it. The letter itself gives you no uncertain picture — no lecturer is needed to stand by with a stick and point out its details and let on to explain what they mean. The picture is the very clear and remorsefully faithful picture of a fallen and fettered angel who is ashamed of himself; an angel who beats his soiled wings and cries, who complains to the woman who enticed him that he *could* have borne his wayward lot, he *could* have stood by his duty if it had not been for her beguilements; an angel who rails at the " boundless ocean of abhorred society," and rages at his poor judicious sister-in-law. If there is any dignity about this spectacle it will escape most people.

Yet when the paragraph of comment is taken as a whole, the picture is full of dignity and pathos; we have before us a blameless and noble spirit stricken to the earth by malign powers, but not conquered; tempted, but grandly putting the temptation away; enmeshed by subtle coils, but sternly resolved to rend them and march forth victorious, at any peril of life or limb. Curtain — slow music.

Was it the purpose of the paragraph to take the bad taste of Shelley's letter out of the reader's mouth? If that was not it, good ink was wasted; without that, it has no relevancy — the multiplication table would have padded the space as rationally.

We have inspected the six reasons which we are asked to believe drove a man of conspicuous patience, honor, justice, fairness, kindliness, and iron firmness, resolution, and steadfastness, from the wife whom he loved and who loved him, to a refuge in the mephitic paradise of Bracknell. These are six infinitely little reasons; but there were six colossal ones, and these the counsel for the destruction of Harriet Shelley persists in not considering very important.

D*.*.

Moreover, the colossal six preceded the little six, and had done the mischief before they were born. Let us double-column the twelve; then we shall see at a glance that each little reason is in turn answered by a retorting reason of a size to overshadow it and make it insignificant:

1. Harriet sets up carriage.	1. CORNELIA TURNER.
2. Harriet stops studying.	2. CORNELIA TURNER.
3. Harriet goes to bonnet-shop.	3. CORNELIA TURNER.
4. Harriet takes a wet-nurse.	4. CORNELIA TURNER.
5. Harriet has too much nerve.	5. CORNELIA TURNER.
6. Detested sister-in-law.	6. CORNELIA TURNER.

As soon as we comprehend that Cornelia Turner and the Italian lessons happened *before* the little six had been discovered to be grievances, we understand why Shelley's happiness in his home had been wounded and bruised almost to death, and no one can persuade us into laying it on Harriet. Shelley and Cornelia are the responsible persons, and we cannot in honor and decency allow the cruelties which they practised upon the unoffending wife to be pushed aside in order to give us a chance to waste time and tears over six sentimental justifications of an offence which the six can't justify, nor even respectably assist in justifying.

Six? There were seven; but in charity to the biographer the seventh ought not to be exposed. Still, he hung it out himself, and not only hung it out, but thought it was a good point in Shelley's favor. For two years Shelley found sympathy and intellectual food and all that at home; there was

enough for spiritual and mental support, but not
enough for luxury; and so, at the end of the contented two years, this latter detail justifies him in
going bag and baggage over to Cornelia Turner and
supplying the rest of his need in the way of surplus
sympathy and intellectual pie unlawfully. By the
same reasoning a man in merely comfortable circumstances may rob a bank without sin.

III

IT is 1814, it is the 16th of March, Shelley has
written his letter, he has been in the Boinville
paradise a month, his deserted wife is in her hus-
bandless home. Mischief had been wrought. It is
the biographer who concedes this. We greatly need
some light on Harriet's side of the case now; we
need to know how she enjoyed the month, but there
is no way to inform ourselves; there seems to be a
strange absence of documents and letters and diaries
on that side. Shelley kept a diary, the approaching
Mary Godwin kept a diary, her father kept one, her
half-sister by marriage, adoption, and the dispensa-
tion of God kept one, and the entire tribe and all its
friends wrote and received letters, and the letters
were kept and are producible when this biography
needs them; but there are only three or four scraps
of Harriet's writing, and no diary. Harriet wrote
plenty of letters to her husband — nobody knows

causes of deep division.   But next comes another
disappointing sentence:

"To guess at the precise nature of these causes, in the absence of
definite statement, were useless."

Why, he has already been guessing at them for
several pages, and we have been trying to outguess
him, and now all of a sudden he is tired of it and
won't play any more.   It is not quite fair to us.
However, he will get over this by-and-by, when
Shelley commits his next indiscretion and has to be
guessed out of it at Harriet's expense.

"We may rest content with Shelley's own
words" — in a Chancery paper drawn up by him
three years later.   They were these: "Delicacy
forbids me to say more than that we were disunited
by incurable dissensions."

As for me, I do not quite see why we should rest
content with anything of the sort.   It is not a very
definite statement.   It does not necessarily mean
anything more than that he did not wish to go into
the tedious details of those family quarrels.   Delicacy could quite properly excuse him from saying,
" I was in love with Cornelia all that time; my wife
kept crying and worrying about it and upbraiding
me and begging me to cut myself free from a connection which was wronging her and disgracing us
both; and I being stung by these reproaches retorted with fierce and bitter speeches — for it is my
nature to do that when I am stirred, especially if
the target of them is a person whom I had greatly

loved and respected before, as witness my various
attitudes towards Miss Hitchener, the Gisbornes,
Harriet's sister, and others — and finally I did not
improve this state of things when I deserted my wife
and spent a whole month with the woman who had
infatuated me.''

No, he could not go into those details, and we
excuse him; but, nevertheless, we do not rest content with this bland proposition to puff away that
whole long disreputable episode with a single mean-
ingless remark of Shelley's.

We do admit that '' it is certain that some cause
or causes of deep division were in operation.'' We
would admit it just the same if the grammar of the
statement were as straight as a string, for we drift
into pretty indifferent grammar ourselves when we
are absorbed in historical work; but we have to decline to admit that we cannot guess those cause or
causes.

But guessing is not really necessary. There is
evidence attainable — evidence from the batch dis-
credited by the biographer and set out at the back
door in his appendix-basket; and yet a court of law
would think twice before throwing it out, whereas it
would be a hardy person who would venture to offer
in such a place a good part of the material which is
placed before the readers of this book as '' evidence,'' and so treated by this daring biographer.
Among some letters (in the appendix-basket) from
Mrs. Godwin, detailing the Godwinian share in the

Then Shelley writes a poem — a chant of grief over the hard fate which obliges him now to leave his paradise and take up with his wife again. It seems to intimate that the paradise is cooling towards him; that he is warned off by acclamation; that he must not even venture to tempt with one last tear his friend Cornelia's ungentle mood, for her eye is glazed and cold and dares not entreat her lover to stay:

Exhibit E

.   .   .   .

" Pause not! the time is past!   Every voice cries ' Away!'
   Tempt not with one last tear thy friend's ungentle mood;
  Thy lover's eye, so glazed and cold, dares not entreat thy stay:
   Duty and dereliction guide thee back to solitude."

Back to the solitude of his now empty home, that is!

   " Away! away! to thy sad and silent home;
   Pour bitter tears on its desolated hearth."

.   .   .   .

But he will have rest in the grave by-and-by. Until that time comes, the charms of Bracknell will remain in his memory, along with Mrs. Boinville's voice and Cornelia Turner's smile:

" Thou in the grave shalt rest — yet, till the phantoms flee
   Which that house and hearth and garden made dear to thee ere-
     while,
  Thy remembrance and repentance and deep musings are not free
   From the music of two voices and the light of one sweet smile."

We *cannot* wonder that Harriet could not stand it. Any of us would have left. We would not even stay with a cat that was in this condition. Even the Boinvilles could not endure it; and so, as we have seen, they gave this one notice.

"Early in May, Shelley was in London. He did not yet despair of reconciliation with Harriet, nor had he ceased to love her."

Shelley's poems are a good deal of trouble to his biographer. They are constantly inserted as " evidence," and they make much confusion. As soon as one of them has proved one thing, another one follows and proves quite a different thing. The poem just quoted shows that he was in love with Cornelia, but a month later he is in love with Harriet again, and there is a poem to prove it.

"In this piteous appeal Shelley declares that he has now no grief but one — the grief of having known and lost his wife's love."

Exhibit F

" Thy look of love has power to calm
The stormiest passion of my soul."

But without doubt she had been reserving her looks of love a good part of the time for ten months, now — ever since he began to lavish his own on Cornelia Turner at the end of the previous July. He does really seem to have already forgotten Cornelia's merits in one brief month, for he eulogizes Harriet in a way which rules all competition out:

" Thou only virtuous, gentle, kind,
Amid a world of hate."

He complains of her hardness, and begs her to make the concession of a " slight endurance " — of his waywardness, perhaps — for the sake of " a

5ᴱ

fellow-being's lasting weal.'' But the main force of his appeal is in his closing stanza, and is strongly worded :

> " O trust for once no erring guide !
>   Bid the remorseless feeling flee;
> 'Tis malice, 'tis revenge, 'tis pride,
>   'Tis anything but thee;
> O deign a nobler pride to prove,
> And pity if thou canst not love.''

This is in May — apparently towards the end of it. Harriet and Shelley were corresponding all the time. Harriet got the poem — a copy exists in her own handwriting; she being the only gentle and kind person amid a world of hate, according to Shelley's own testimony in the poem, we are permitted to think that the daily letters would presently have melted that kind and gentle heart and brought about the reconciliation, if there had been time — but there wasn't; for in a very few days — in fact, before the 8th of June — Shelley was in love with *another* woman.

And so — perhaps while Harriet was walking the floor nights, trying to get *her* poem by heart — her husband was doing a fresh one — for the other girl — Mary Wollstonecraft Godwin — with sentiments like these in it:

Exhibit G

> " To spend years thus and be rewarded,
>   As thou, sweet love, requited me
>   When none were near.
>   . . . thy lips did meet
>   Mine tremblingly; . . .

" Gentle and good and mild thou art,
    Nor can I live if thou appear
    Aught but thyself." . . .

And so on. " Before the close of June it was known
and felt by Mary and Shelley that each was inex-
pressibly dear to the other." Yes, Shelley had
found this child of sixteen to his liking, and had
wooed and won her in the graveyard. But that is
nothing; it was better than wooing her in her
nursery, at any rate, where it might have disturbed
the other children.

However, she was a child in years only. From
the day that she set her masculine grip on Shelley
he was to frisk no more. If she had occupied the
only kind and gentle Harriet's place in March it
would have been a thrilling spectacle to see her in-
vade the Boinville rookery and read the riot act.
That holiday of Shelley's would have been of short
duration, and Cornelia's hair would have been as
gray as her mother's when the services were over.

Hogg went to the Godwin residence in Skinner
Street with Shelley on that 8th of June. They
passed through Godwin's little debt-factory of a
book-shop and went up-stairs hunting for the pro-
prietor. Nobody there. Shelley strode about the
room impatiently, making its crazy floor quake under
him. Then a door " was partially and softly opened.
A thrilling voice called ' Shelley !' A thrilling voice
answered, ' Mary !' And he darted out of the room
like an arrow from the bow of the far-shooting King.

A very young female, fair and fair-haired, pale, indeed, and with a piercing look, wearing a frock of tartan, an unusual dress in London at that time, had called him out of the room.''

This is Mary Godwin, as described by Hogg. The thrill of the voices shows that the love of Shelley and Mary was already upward of a fortnight old; therefore it had been born within the month of May — born while Harriet was still trying to get her poem by heart, we think. I must not be asked how I know so much about that thrill; it is my secret. The biographer and I have private ways of finding out things when it is necessary to find them out and the customary methods fail.

Shelley left London that day, and was gone ten days. The biographer conjectures that he spent this interval with Harriet in Bath. It would be just like him. To the end of his days he liked to be in love with two women at once. He was more in love with Miss Hitchener when he married Harriet than he was with Harriet, and told the lady so with simple and unostentatious candor. He was more in love with Cornelia than he was with Harriet in the end of 1813 and the beginning of 1814, yet he supplied both of them with love poems of an equal temperature meantime; he loved Mary and Harriet in June, and while getting ready to run off with the one, it is conjectured that he put in his odd time trying to get reconciled to the other; by-and-by, while still in love with Mary, he will make love to her half-sister by marriage, adoption, and the visitation of God, through the medium of clandestine letters, and she will answer with letters that are for no eye but his own.

When Shelley encountered Mary Godwin he was looking around for another paradise. He had tastes of his own, and there were features about the Godwin establishment that strongly recommended it. Godwin was an advanced thinker and an able writer. One of his romances is still read, but his philosophical works, once so esteemed, are out of vogue now; their authority was already declining when Shelley made his acquaintance — that is, it was declining with the public, but not with Shelley. They had been his moral and political Bible, and they were that yet. Shelley the infidel would himself have claimed to be less a work of God than a work of Godwin. Godwin's philosophies had formed his mind and interwoven themselves into it and become a part of its texture; he regarded himself as Godwin's spiritual son. Godwin was not without self-appreciation; indeed, it may be conjectured that from his point of view the last syllable of his name was surplusage. He lived serene in his lofty world of philosophy, far above the mean interests that absorbed smaller men, and only came down to the ground at intervals to pass the hat for alms to pay his debts with, and insult the man that relieved him. Several of his principles were out of the ordinary. For example, he was opposed to marriage. He was

5*₊*₊

not aware that his preachings from this text were but theory and wind; he supposed he was in earnest in imploring people to live together without marrying, until Shelley furnished him a working model of his scheme and a practical example to analyze, by applying the principle in his own family; the matter took a different and surprising aspect then. The late Matthew Arnold said that the main defect in Shelley's make-up was that he was destitute of the sense of humor. This episode must have escaped Mr. Arnold's attention.

But we have said enough about the head of the new paradise. Mrs. Godwin is described as being in several ways a terror; and even when her soul was in repose she wore green spectacles. But I suspect that her main unattractiveness was born of the fact that she wrote the letters that are out in the appendix-basket in the back yard — letters which are an outrage and wholly untrustworthy, for they say some kind things about poor Harriet and tell some disagreeable truths about her husband; and these things make the fabulist grit his teeth a good deal.

Next we have Fanny Godwin — a Godwin by courtesy only; she was Mrs. Godwin's natural daughter by a former friend. She was a sweet and winning girl, but she presently wearied of the Godwin paradise, and poisoned herself.

Last in the list is Jane (or Claire, as she preferred to call herself) Clairmont, daughter of Mrs. Godwin

by a former marriage. She was very young and
pretty and accommodating, and always ready to do
what she could to make things pleasant. After
Shelley ran off with her part-sister Mary, she became the guest of the pair, and contributed a natural
child to their nursery — Allegra. Lord Byron was
the father.

We have named the several members and advan-
tages of the new paradise in Skinner Street, with its
crazy book-shop underneath. Shelley was all right
now, this was a better place than the other; more
variety anyway, and more different kinds of fra-
grance. One could turn out poetry here without
any trouble at all.

The way the new love-match came about was this:
Shelley told Mary all his aggravations and sorrows
and griefs, and about the wet-nurse and the bonnet-
shop and the surgeon and the carriage, and the
sister-in-law that blocked the London game, and
about Cornelia and her mamma, and how they had
turned him out of the house after making so much
of him; and how he had deserted Harriet and then
Harriet had deserted him, and how the reconciliation
was working along and Harriet getting her poem by
heart; and still he was not happy, and Mary pitied
him, for she had had trouble herself. But I am not
satisfied with this. It reads too much like statistics.
It lacks smoothness and grace, and is too earthy and
business-like. It has the sordid look of a trades-
union procession out on strike. That is not the

E*₊*₊

right form for it. The book does it better; we will fall back on the book and have a cake-walk:

> "It was easy to divine that some restless grief possessed him; Mary herself was not unlearned in the lore of pain. His generous zeal in her father's behalf, his spiritual sonship to Godwin, his reverence for her mother's memory, were guarantees with Mary of his excellence.* The new friends could not lack subjects of discourse, and underneath their words about Mary's mother, and 'Political Justice,' and 'Rights of Woman,' were two young hearts, each feeling towards the other, each perhaps unaware, trembling in the direction of the other. The desire to assuage the suffering of one whose happiness has grown precious to us may become a hunger of the spirit as keen as any other, and this hunger now possessed Mary's heart; when her eyes rested unseen on Shelley, it was with a look full of the ardor of a 'soothing pity.'"

Yes, that is better and has more composure. That is just the way it happened. He told her about the wet-nurse, she told him about political justice; he told her about the deadly sister-in-law, she told him about her mother; he told her about the bonnet-shop, she murmured back about the rights of woman; then he assuaged her, then she assuaged him; then he assuaged her some more, next she assuaged him some more; then they both assuaged one another simultaneously; and so they went on by the hour assuaging and assuaging and assuaging, until at last what was the result? They were in love. It will happen so every time.

> "He had married a woman who, as he now persuaded himself, had never truly loved him, who loved only his fortune and his rank, and who proved her selfishness by deserting him in his misery."

---

* What she was after was guarantees of his excellence. That he stood ready to desert his wife and child was one of them, apparently.

I think that that is not quite fair to Harriet. We have no certainty that she knew Cornelia had turned him out of the house. He went back to Cornelia, and Harriet may have supposed that he was as happy with her as ever. Still, it was judicious to begin to lay on the whitewash, for Shelley is going to need many a coat of it now, and the sooner the reader becomes used to the intrusion of the brush the sooner he will get reconciled to it and stop fretting about it.

After Shelley's (conjectured) visit to Harriet at Bath — 8th of June to 18th — "it seems to have been arranged that Shelley should henceforth join the Skinner Street household each day at dinner."

Nothing could be handier than this; things will swim along now.

"Although now Shelley was coming to believe that his wedded union with Harriet was a thing of the past, he had not ceased to regard her with affectionate consideration ; he wrote to her frequently, and kept her informed of his whereabouts."

We must not get impatient over these curious inharmoniousnesses and irreconcilabilities in Shelley's character. You can see by the biographer's attitude towards them that there is nothing objectionable about them. Shelley was doing his best to make two adoring young creatures happy: he was regarding the one with affectionate consideration by mail, and he was assuaging the other one at home.

"Unhappy Harriet, residing at Bath, had perhaps never desired that

Coliseum of conjectures built out of a waste-basket
of poetry. For we have " evidence " now — not
poetry and conjecture. When Shelley had been
dining daily in the Skinner Street paradise fifteen
days and continuing the love-match which was
already a fortnight old twenty-five days earlier, he
forgot to write Harriet; forgot it the next day and
the next. During four days Harriet got no letter
from him. Then her fright and anxiety rose to
expression-heat, and she wrote a letter to Shelley's
publisher which seems to reveal to us that Shelley's
letters to her had been the customary affectionate
letters of husband to wife, and had carried no appeals for reconciliation and had not needed to:

> "BATH (postmark July 7, 1814).
>
> "MY DEAR SIR,—You will greatly oblige me by giving the enclosed
> to Mr. Shelley. I would not trouble you, but it is now four days since
> I have heard from him, which to me is an age. Will you write by re-
> turn of post and tell me what has become of him ? as I always fancy
> something dreadful has happened if I do not hear from him. If you
> tell me that he is well I shall not come to London, but if I do not hear
> from you or him I shall certainly come, as I cannot endure this dreadful
> state of suspense. You are his friend and you can feel for me.
>
> "I remain yours truly,
>
> "H. S."

Even without Peacock's testimony that " her whole
aspect and demeanor were manifest emanations of a
pure and truthful nature," we should hold this to
be a truthful letter, a sincere letter, a loving letter;
it bears those marks; I think it is also the letter of
a person accustomed to receiving letters from her

husband frequently, and that they have been of a welcome and satisfactory sort, too, this long time back — ever since the solemn remarriage and reconciliation at the altar most likely.

The biographer follows Harriet's letter with a conjecture. He conjectures that she " would now gladly have retraced her steps.'' Which means that it is proven that she had steps to retrace — proven by the poem. Well, if the poem is better evidence than the letter, we must let it stand at that.

Then the biographer attacks Harriet Shelley's honor — by authority of random and unverified gossip scavengered from a group of people whose very names make a person shudder: Mary Godwin, mistress to Shelley; her part-sister, discarded mistress of Lord Byron; Godwin, the philosophical tramp, who gathers his share of it from a shadow — that is to say, from a person whom he shirks out of naming. Yet the biographer dignifies this sorry rubbish with the name of '' evidence.''

Nothing remotely resembling a distinct charge from a named person professing to know is offered among this precious '' evidence.''

1. '' Shelley *believed* '' so and so.

2. Byron's discarded mistress says that Shelley told Mary Godwin so and so, and *Mary* told *her*.

3. '' Shelley said '' so and so — and later '' admitted over and over again that he had been in error.''

4. The unspeakable Godwin '' wrote to Mr. Bax-

something over two months later.   The truants were back in London before either of these events occurred.

On one occasion, presently, Shelley was so pressed for money to support his mistress with that he went to his wife and got some money of his that was in her hands — twenty pounds.   Yet the mistress was not moved to gratitude; for later, when the wife was troubled to meet her engagements, the mistress makes this entry in her diary:

"Harriet sends her creditors here; nasty woman.   Now we shall have to change our lodgings."

The deserted wife bore the bitterness and obloquy of her situation two years and a quarter; then she gave up, and drowned herself.   A month afterwards the body was found in the water.   Three weeks later Shelley married his mistress.

I must here be allowed to italicize a remark of the biographer's concerning Harriet Shelley:

"*That no act of Shelley's during the two years which immediately preceded her death tended to cause the rash act which brought her life to its close seems certain.*"

Yet her husband had deserted her and her children, and was living with a concubine all that time! Why should a person attempt to write biography when the simplest facts have no meaning to him? This book is littered with as crass stupidities as that one — deductions by the page which bear no discoverable kinship to their premises.

The biographer throws off that extraordinary remark without any perceptible disturbance to his serenity; for he follows it with a sentimental justification of Shelley's conduct which has not a pang of conscience in it, but is silky and smooth and undulating and pious — a cake-walk with all the colored brethren at their best. There may be people who can read that page and keep their temper, but it is doubtful.

Shelley's life has the one indelible blot upon it, but is otherwise worshipfully noble and beautiful. It even stands out indestructibly gracious and lovely from the ruck of these disastrous pages, in spite of the fact that they expose and establish his responsibility for his forsaken wife's pitiful fate — a responsibility which he himself tacitly admits in a letter to Eliza Westbrook, wherein he refers to his taking up with Mary Godwin as an act which Eliza " might excusably regard as the cause of her sister's ruin."

6E

the neighborhood of the subject in hand, and be interesting to the reader, and help out the tale, and stop when the people cannot think of anything more to say. But this requirement has been ignored from the beginning of the *Deerslayer* tale to the end of it.

6. They require that when the author describes the character of a personage in his tale, the conduct and conversation of that personage shall justify said description. But this law gets little or no attention in the *Deerslayer* tale, as Natty Bumppo's case will amply prove.

7. They require that when a personage talks like an illustrated, gilt-edged, tree-calf, hand-tooled, seven-dollar Friendship's Offering in the beginning of a paragraph, he shall not talk like a negro minstrel in the end of it. But this rule is flung down and danced upon in the *Deerslayer* tale.

8. They require that crass stupidities shall not be played upon the reader as " the craft of the woodsman, the delicate art of the forest," by either the author or the people in the tale. But this rule is persistently violated in the *Deerslayer* tale.

9. They require that the personages of a tale shall confine themselves to possibilities and let miracles alone; or, if they venture a miracle, the author must so plausibly set it forth as to make it look possible and reasonable. But these rules are not respected in the *Deerslayer* tale.

10. They require that the author shall make the reader feel a deep interest in the personages of his

tale and in their fate; and that he shall make the reader love the good people in the tale and hate the bad ones. But the reader of the *Deerslayer* tale dislikes the good people in it, is indifferent to the others, and wishes they would all get drowned together.

11. They require that the characters in a tale shall be so clearly defined that the reader can tell beforehand what each will do in a given emergency. But in the *Deerslayer* tale this rule is vacated.

In addition to these large rules there are some little ones. These require that the author shall

12. *Say* what he is proposing to say, not merely come near it.

13. Use the right word, not its second cousin.

14. Eschew surplusage.

15. Not omit necessary details.

16. Avoid slovenliness of form.

17. Use good grammar.

18. Employ a simple and straightforward style.

Even these seven are coldly and persistently violated in the *Deerslayer* tale.

Cooper's gift in the way of invention was not a rich endowment; but such as it was he liked to work it, he was pleased with the effects, and indeed he did some quite sweet things with it. In his little box of stage properties he kept six or eight cunning devices, tricks, artifices for his savages and woodsmen to deceive and circumvent each other with, and he was never so happy as when he was working

6*₊*₊

these innocent things and seeing them go. A favorite one was to make a moccasined person tread in the tracks of the moccasined enemy, and thus hide his own trail. Cooper wore out barrels and barrels of moccasins in working that trick. Another stage-property that he pulled out of his box pretty frequently was his broken twig. He prized his broken twig above all the rest of his effects, and worked it the hardest. It is a restful chapter in any book of his when somebody doesn't step on a dry twig and alarm all the reds and whites for two hundred yards around. Every time a Cooper person is in peril, and absolute silence is worth four dollars a minute, he is sure to step on a dry twig. There may be a hundred handier things to step on, but that wouldn't satisfy Cooper. Cooper requires him to turn out and find a dry twig; and if he can't do it, go and borrow one. In fact, the Leather Stocking Series ought to have been called the Broken Twig Series.

I am sorry there is not room to put in a few dozen instances of the delicate art of the forest, as practised by Natty Bumppo and some of the other Cooperian experts. Perhaps we may venture two or three samples. Cooper was a sailor — a naval officer; yet he gravely tells us how a vessel, driving towards a lee shore in a gale, is steered for a particular spot by her skipper because he knows of an *undertow* there which will hold her back against the gale and save her. For just pure woodcraft, or sailorcraft, or whatever it is, isn't that neat? For several years Cooper was daily in the society of artillery, and he ought to have noticed that when a cannon-ball strikes the ground it either buries itself or skips a hundred feet or so; skips again a hundred feet or so — and so on, till finally it gets tired and rolls. Now in one place he loses some "females" — as he always calls women — in the edge of a wood near a plain at night in a fog, on purpose to give Bumppo a chance to show off the delicate art of the forest before the reader. These mislaid people are hunting for a fort. They hear a cannon-blast, and a cannon-ball presently comes rolling into the wood and stops at their feet. To the females this suggests nothing. The case is very different with the admirable Bumppo. I wish I may never know peace again if he doesn't strike out promptly and *follow the track* of that cannon-ball across the plain through the dense fog and find the fort. Isn't it a daisy? If Cooper had any real knowledge of Nature's ways of doing things, he had a most delicate art in concealing the fact. For instance: one of his acute Indian experts, Chingachgook (pronounced Chicago, I think), has lost the trail of a person he is tracking through the forest. Apparently that trail is hopelessly lost. Neither you nor I could ever have guessed out the way to find it. It was very different with Chicago. Chicago was not stumped for long. He turned a running stream out of its course, and there, in the slush in its old

F*_**_*

bed, were that person's moccasin-tracks. The current did not wash them away, as it would have done in all other like cases — no, even the eternal laws of Nature have to vacate when Cooper wants to put up a delicate job of woodcraft on the reader.

We must be a little wary when Brander Matthews tells us that Cooper's books " reveal an extraordinary fulness of invention." As a rule, I am quite willing to accept Brander Matthews's literary judgments and applaud his lucid and graceful phrasing of them; but that particular statement needs to be taken with a few tons of salt. Bless your heart, Cooper hadn't any more invention than a horse; and I don't mean a high-class horse, either; I mean a clothes-horse. It would be very difficult to find a really clever " situation " in Cooper's books, and still more difficult to find one of any kind which he has failed to render absurd by his handling of it. Look at the episodes of " the caves "; and at the celebrated scuffle between Maqua and those others on the table-land a few days later; and at Hurry Harry's queer water-transit from the castle to the ark; and at Deerslayer's half-hour with his first corpse; and at the quarrel between Hurry Harry and Deerslayer later; and at — but choose for yourself; you can't go amiss.

If Cooper had been an observer his inventive faculty would have worked better; not more interestingly, but more rationally, more plausibly. Cooper's proudest creations in the way of " situations " suffer

noticeably from the absence of the observer's protecting gift. Cooper's eye was splendidly inaccurate.
Cooper seldom saw anything correctly. He saw
nearly all things as through a glass eye, darkly. Of
course a man who cannot see the commonest little
every-day matters accurately is working at a disad-
vantage when he is constructing a " situation." In
the *Deerslayer* tale Cooper has a stream which is
fifty feet wide where it flows out of a lake; it
presently narrows to twenty as it meanders along
for no given reason, and yet when a stream acts like
that it ought to be required to explain itself. Four-
teen pages later the width of the brook's outlet from
the lake has suddenly shrunk thirty feet, and become " the narrowest part of the stream." This
shrinkage is not accounted for. The stream has
bends in it, a sure indication that it has alluvial
banks and cuts them; yet these bends are only
thirty and fifty feet long. If Cooper had been a
nice and punctilious observer he would have noticed
that the bends were oftener nine hundred feet long
than short of it.

Cooper made the exit of that stream fifty feet
wide, in the first place, for no particular reason; in
the second place, he narrowed it to less than twenty
to accommodate some Indians. He bends a " sap-
ling " to the form of an arch over this narrow
passage, and conceals six Indians in its foliage.
They are " laying " for a settler's scow or ark
which is coming up the stream on its way to the

The boat has passed under and is now out of their reach. Let me explain what the five did — you would not be able to reason it out for yourself. No. 1 jumped for the boat, but fell in the water astern of it. Then No. 2 jumped for the boat, but fell in the water still farther astern of it. Then No. 3 jumped for the boat, and fell a good way astern of it. Then No. 4 jumped for the boat, and fell in the water *away* astern. Then even No. 5 made a jump for the boat — for he was a Cooper Indian. In the matter of intellect, the difference between a Cooper Indian and the Indian that stands in front of the cigar-shop is not spacious. The scow episode is really a sublime burst of invention; but it does not thrill, because the inaccuracy of the details throws a sort of air of fictitiousness and general improbability over it. This comes of Cooper's inadequacy as an observer.

The reader will find some examples of Cooper's high talent for inaccurate observation in the account of the shooting-match in *The Pathfinder*.

"A common wrought nail was driven lightly into the target, its head having been first touched with paint."

The color of the paint is not stated — an important omission, but Cooper deals freely in important omissions. No, after all, it was not an important omission; for this nail-head is *a hundred yards from* the marksmen, and could not be seen by them at that distance, no matter what its color might be.

How far can the best eyes see a common house-fly?
A hundred yards? It is quite impossible. Very
well; eyes that cannot see a house-fly that is a hundred yards away cannot see an ordinary nail-head at
that distance, for the size of the two objects is the
same. It takes a keen eye to see a fly or a nail-
head at fifty yards — one hundred and fifty feet.
Can the reader do it?

The nail was lightly driven, its head painted, and
game called. Then the Cooper miracles began. The
bullet of the first marksman chipped an edge of the
nail-head; the next man's bullet drove the nail a
little way into the target — and removed all the
paint. Haven't the miracles gone far enough now?
Not to suit Cooper; for the purpose of this whole
scheme is to show off his prodigy, Deerslayer-
Hawkeye - Long - Rifle-Leather-Stocking-Pathfinder-
Bumppo before the ladies.

" ' Be all ready to clench it, boys! ' cried out Pathfinder, stepping
into his friend's tracks the instant they were vacant. ' Never mind a
new nail; I can see that, though the paint is gone, and what I can see
I can hit at a hundred yards, though it were only a mosquito's eye. Be
ready to clench! '

"The rifle cracked, the bullet sped its way, and the head of the nail
was buried in the wood, covered by the piece of flattened lead."

There, you see, is a man who could hunt flies
with a rifle, and command a ducal salary in a Wild
West show to-day if we had him back with us.

The recorded feat is certainly surprising just as it
stands; but it is not surprising enough for Cooper.

Is the miracle sufficient as it stands? Not for Cooper. The Pathfinder speaks again, as he " now slowly advances towards the stage occupied by the females ":

> " ' That's not all, boys, that's not all; if you find the target touched at all, I'll own to a miss. The Quartermaster cut the wood, but you'll find no wood cut by that last messenger."

The miracle is at last complete. He knew — doubtless *saw* — at the distance of a hundred yards — that his bullet had passed into the hole *without fraying the edges*. There were now three bullets in that one hole — three bullets embedded procession-ally in the body of the stump back of the target. Everybody knew this — somehow or other — and yet nobody had dug any of them out to make sure. Cooper is not a close observer, but he is interesting. He is certainly always that, no matter what happens. And he is more interesting when he is not noticing what he is about than when he is. This is a con-siderable merit.

The conversations in the Cooper books have a curious sound in our modern ears. To believe that such talk really ever came out of people's mouths would be to believe that there was a time when time was of no value to a person who thought he had something to say; when it was the custom to spread a two-minute remark out to ten; when a man's mouth was a rolling-mill, and busied itself all day long in turning four-foot pigs of thought into thirty-foot bars of conversational railroad iron by attenuation; when subjects were seldom faithfully stuck to, but the talk wandered all around and arrived nowhere; when conversations consisted mainly of irrelevancies, with here and there a relevancy, a relevancy with an embarrassed look, as not being able to explain how it got there.

Cooper was certainly not a master in the construction of dialogue. Inaccurate observation defeated him here as it defeated him in so many other enterprises of his. He even failed to notice that the man who talks corrupt English six days in the week must and will talk it on the seventh, and can't help himself. In the *Deerslayer* story he lets Deerslayer talk the showiest kind of book-talk sometimes, and at other times the basest of base dialects. For instance, when some one asks him if he has a sweetheart, and if so, where she abides, this is his majestic answer:

"'She's in the forest — hanging from the boughs of the trees, in a soft rain — in the dew on the open grass — the clouds that float about in the blue heavens — the birds that sing in the woods — the sweet springs where I slake my thirst — and in all the other glorious gifts that come from God's Providence!'"

And he preceded that, a little before, with this:

"'It consarns me as all things that touches a fri'nd consarns a fri'nd.'"

And this is another of his remarks:

"'If I was Injin born, now, I might tell of this, or carry in the scalp and boast of the expl'ite afore the whole tribe; or if my inimy had only been a bear'"— and so on.

7 E

We cannot imagine such a thing as a veteran
Scotch Commander-in-Chief comporting himself in
the field like a windy melodramatic actor, but
Cooper could.   On one occasion Alice and Cora
were being chased by the French through a fog in
the neighborhood of their father's fort:

> " '*Point de quartier aux coquins!* ' cried an eager pursuer, who
> seemed to direct the operations of the enemy.
>
> " ' Stand firm and be ready, my gallant 60ths! ' suddenly exclaimed
> a voice above them; ' wait to see the enemy; fire low, and sweep the
> glacis.'
>
> " ' Father! father! ' exclaimed a piercing cry from out the mist; ' it
> is I! Alice! thy own Elsie! spare, O! save your daughters! '
>
> " ' Hold! ' shouted the former speaker, in the awful tones of parental
> agony, the sound reaching even to the woods, and rolling back in solemn
> echo.   ' 'Tis she!   God has restored me my children!   Throw open
> the sally-port; to the field, 60ths, to the field! pull not a trigger, lest ye
> kill my lambs!   Drive off these dogs of France with your steel! ' "

Cooper's word-sense was singularly dull.   When
a person has a poor ear for music he will flat and
sharp right along without knowing it.   He keeps
near the tune, but it is *not* the tune.   When a person
has a poor ear for words, the result is a literary flatting and sharping; you perceive what he is intending to say, but you also perceive that he doesn't
say it.   This is Cooper.   He was not a word-
musician.   His ear was satisfied with the *approxi-
mate* word.   I will furnish some circumstantial
evidence in support of this charge.   My instances
are gathered from half a dozen pages of the tale
called *Deerslayer*.   He uses " verbal," for " oral ";
" precision," for " facility "; " phenomena," for

" marvels " ; " necessary," for " predetermined " ;
" unsophisticated," for " primitive " ; " prepara-
tion," for " expectancy " ; " rebuked," for " subdued " ; " dependent on," for " resulting from " ;
" fact," for " condition " ; " fact," for " conjecture " ; " precaution," for " caution " ; " explain,"
for " determine " ; " mortified," for " disappointed" ; "meretricious," for "factitious" ; "ma-
terially," for " considerably " ; " decreasing," for
" deepening " ; " increasing," for " disappearing " ;
" embedded," for " enclosed " ; " treacherous,"
for " hostile " ; " stood," for " stooped " ; " softened," for " replaced " ; " rejoined," for " remarked " ; " situation," for " condition " ; " different," for " differing " ; " insensible," for
" unsentient " ; " brevity," for " celerity " ; " dis-
trusted," for " suspicious " ; " mental imbecility,"
for " imbecility " ; " eyes," for " sight " ; " coun-
teracting," for " opposing " ; " funeral obsequies,"
for " obsequies."

There have been daring people in the world who
claimed that Cooper could write English, but they
are all dead now — all dead but Lounsbury. I don't
remember that Lounsbury makes the claim in so
many words, still he makes it, for he says that *Deerslayer* is a " pure work of art." Pure, in that connection, means faultless — faultless in all details —
and language is a detail. If Mr. Lounsbury had
only compared Cooper's English with the English
which he writes himself — but it is plain that he

didn't; and so it is likely that he imagines until this day that Cooper's is as clean and compact as his own. Now I feel sure, deep down in my heart, that Cooper wrote about the poorest English that exists in our language, and that the English of *Deerslayer* is the very worst that even Cooper ever wrote.

I may be mistaken, but it does seem to me that *Deerslayer* is not a work of art in any sense; it does seem to me that it is destitute of every detail that goes to the making of a work of art; in truth, it seems to me that *Deerslayer* is just simply a literary *delirium tremens*.

A work of art? It has no invention; it has no order, system, sequence, or result; it has no life-likeness, no thrill, no stir, no seeming of reality; its characters are confusedly drawn, and by their acts and words they prove that they are not the sort of people the author claims that they are; its humor is pathetic; its pathos is funny; its conversations are — oh! indescribable; its love-scenes odious; its English a crime against the language.

Counting these out, what is left is Art. I think we must all admit that.

TRAVELING WITH A REFORMER

LAST spring I went out to Chicago to see the Fair, and although I did not see it my trip was not wholly lost — there were compensations. In New York I was introduced to a major in the regular army who said he was going to the Fair, and we agreed to go together. I had to go to Boston first, but that did not interfere; he said he would go along, and put in the time. He was a handsome man, and built like a gladiator. But his ways were gentle, and his speech was soft and persuasive. He was companionable, but exceedingly reposeful. Yes, and wholly destitute of the sense of humor. He was full of interest in everything that went on around him, but his serenity was indestructible; nothing disturbed him, nothing excited him.

But before the day was done I found that deep down in him somewhere he had a passion, quiet as he was — a passion for reforming petty public abuses. He stood for citizenship — it was his hobby. His idea was that every citizen of the republic ought to consider himself an unofficial policeman, and keep unsalaried watch and ward over the laws and their execution. He thought that the only

7*.*.   (97)

effective way of preserving and protecting public rights was for each citizen to do his share in preventing or punishing such infringements of them as came under his personal notice.

It was a good scheme, but I thought it would keep a body in trouble all the time; it seemed to me that one would be always trying to get offending little officials discharged, and perhaps getting laughed at for all reward. But he said no, I had the wrong idea; that there was no occasion to get anybody discharged; that in fact you *mustn't* get anybody discharged; that that would itself be a failure; no, one must reform the man — reform him and make him useful where he was.

" Must one report the offender and then beg his superior not to discharge him, but reprimand him and keep him?"

" No, that is not the idea; you don't report him at all, for then you risk his bread and butter. You can act as if you are *going* to report him — when nothing else will answer. But that's an extreme case. That is a sort of *force*, and force is bad. Diplomacy is the effective thing. Now if a man has tact — if a man will exercise diplomacy — "

For two minutes we had been standing at a telegraph wicket, and during all this time the Major had been trying to get the attention of one of the young operators, but they were all busy skylarking. The Major spoke now, and asked one of them to take his telegram. He got for reply:

" I reckon you can wait a minute, can't you?" and the skylarking went on.

The Major said yes, he was not in a hurry. Then he wrote another telegram:

"President Western Union Tel. Co.:

" Come and dine with me this evening. I can tell you how business is conducted in one of your branches."

Presently the young fellow who had spoken so pertly a little before reached out and took the telegram, and when he read it he lost color and began to apologize and explain. He said he would lose his place if this deadly telegram was sent, and he might never get another. If he could be let off this time he would give no cause of complaint again. The compromise was accepted.

As we walked away, the Major said:

" Now, you see, that was diplomacy — and you see how it worked. It wouldn't do any good to bluster, the way people are always doing — that boy can always give you as good as you send, and you'll come out defeated and ashamed of yourself pretty nearly always. But you see he stands no chance against diplomacy. Gentle words and diplomacy — those are the tools to work with."

" Yes, I see; but everybody wouldn't have had your opportunity. It isn't everybody that is on those familiar terms with the president of the Western Union."

" Oh, you misunderstand. I don't know the president — I only use him diplomatically. It is for

G*.*.

his good and for the public good.   There's no harm
in it.''

I said, with hesitation and diffidence:

" But is it ever right or noble to tell a lie?''

He took no note of the delicate self-righteousness
of the question, but answered, with undisturbed
gravity and simplicity:

" Yes, sometimes.   Lies told to injure a person,
and lies told to profit yourself are not justifiable, but
lies told to help another person, and lies told in the
public interest — oh, well, that is quite another
matter.   Anybody knows that.   But never mind
about the methods: you see the result.   That youth
is going to be useful now, and well-behaved.   He
had a good face.   He was worth saving.   Why, he
was worth saving on his mother's account if not his
own.   Of course, he has a mother — sisters, too.
Damn these people who are always forgetting that!
Do you know, I've never fought a duel in my life —
never once — and yet have been challenged, like
other people.   I could always see the other man's
unoffending women folks or his little children standing between him and me.   *They* hadn't done anything — I couldn't break *their* hearts, you know.''

He corrected a good many little abuses in the
course of the day, and always without friction —
always with a fine and dainty " diplomacy '' which
left no sting behind; and he got such happiness and
such contentment out of these performances that I
was obliged to envy him his trade — and perhaps

would have adopted it if I could have managed the necessary deflections from fact as confidently with my mouth as I believe I could with a pen, behind the shelter of print, after a little practice.

Away late that night we were coming up-town in a horse-car when three boisterous roughs got aboard, and began to fling hilarious obscenities and profanities right and left among the timid passengers, some of whom were women and children. Nobody resisted or retorted; the conductor tried soothing words and moral suasion, but the roughs only called him names and laughed at him. Very soon I saw that the Major realized that this was a matter which was in his line; evidently he was turning over his stock of diplomacy in his mind and getting ready. I felt that the first diplomatic remark he made in this place would bring down a land-slide of ridicule upon him and maybe something worse; but before I could whisper to him and check him he had begun, and it was too late. He said, in a level and dispassionate tone:

"Conductor, you must put these swine out. I will help you."

I was not looking for that. In a flash the three roughs plunged at him. But none of them arrived. He delivered three such blows as one could not expect to encounter outside the prize-ring, and neither of the men had life enough left in him to get up from where he fell. The Major dragged them out and threw them off the car, and we got under way again.

" Conductor, where does one report the mis-
conduct of a brakeman? Does one report to you?"

" You can report him at New Haven if you want
to. What has he been doing?"

The Major told the story. The conductor seemed
amused. He said, with just a touch of sarcasm in
his bland tones:

" As I understand you, the brakeman didn't *say*
anything."

" No, he didn't say anything."

" But he scowled, you say."

" Yes."

" And snatched the door loose in a rough way."

" Yes."

" That's the whole business, is it ?"

" Yes, that is the whole of it."

The conductor smiled pleasantly, and said:

" Well, if you want to report him, all right, but I
don't quite make out what it's going to amount to.
You'll say — as I understand you — that the brakeman insulted this old gentleman. They'll ask you
what he *said*. You'll say he didn't say anything at
all. I reckon they'll say, how are you going to
make out an insult when you acknowledge yourself
that he didn't say a word."

There was a murmur of applause at the conductor's compact reasoning, and it gave him pleasure — you could see it in his face. But the Major
was not disturbed. He said:

" There — now you have touched upon a crying

defect in the complaint-system. The railway officials — as the public think and as you also seem to
think — are not aware that there are any kind of
insults except *spoken* ones. So nobody goes to
headquarters and reports insults of manner, insults
of gesture, look, and so forth; and yet these are
sometimes harder to bear than any words. They
are bitter hard to bear because there is nothing
tangible to take hold of; and the insulter can always
say, if called before the railway officials, that he
never dreamed of intending any offence. It seems
to me that the officials ought to specially and
urgently request the public to report *unworded*
affronts and incivilities."

The conductor laughed, and said:

"Well, that *would* be trimming it pretty fine,
sure!"

"But not too fine, I think. I will report this
matter at New Haven, and I have an idea that I'll
be thanked for it."

The conductor's face lost something of its com-
placency; in fact, it settled to a quite sober cast as
the owner of it moved away. I said:

"You are not really going to bother with that
trifle, are you?"

"It isn't a trifle. Such things ought always to
be reported. It is a public duty, and no citizen has
a right to shirk it. But I sha'n't have to report this
case."

"Why?"

" If you would stop and think a moment you wouldn't ask such a question as that. Is a brake-man a dog, that nothing but dog's methods will do for him? He is a man, and has a man's fight for life. And he always has a sister, or a mother, or wife and children to support. Always — there are no exceptions. When you take his living away from him you take theirs away too — and what have they done to you? Nothing. And where is the profit in discharging an uncourteous brakeman and hiring another just like him? It's unwisdom. Don't you see that the rational thing to do is to *reform* the brakeman and keep him? Of course it is."

Then he quoted with admiration the conduct of a certain division superintendent of the Consolidated road, in a case where a switchman of two years' experience was negligent once and threw a train off the track and killed several people. Citizens came in a passion to urge the man's dismissal, but the superintendent said:

" No, you are wrong. He has learned his lesson, he will throw no more trains off the track. He is twice as valuable as he was before. I shall keep him."

We had only one more adventure on the trip. Between Hartford and Springfield the train-boy came shouting in with an armful of literature and dropped a sample into a slumbering gentleman's lap, and the man woke up with a start. He was very angry, and he and a couple of friends discussed the outrage

with much heat.   They sent for the parlor-car conductor and described the matter, and were determined to have the boy expelled from his situation.
The three complainants were wealthy Holyoke merchants, and it was evident that the conductor stood
in some awe of them.   He tried to pacify them,
and explained that the boy was not under his
authority, but under that of one of the news companies; but he accomplished nothing.

Then the Major volunteered some testimony for
the defence.   He said:

" I saw it all.   You gentlemen have not meant to
exaggerate the circumstances, but still that is what
you have done.   The boy has done nothing more
than all train-boys do.   If you want to get his ways
softened down and his manners reformed, I am with
you and ready to help, but it isn't fair to get him
discharged without giving him a chance."

But they were angry, and would hear of no compromise.   They were well acquainted with the president of the Boston & Albany, they said, and would
put everything aside next day and go up to Boston
and fix that boy.

The Major said he would be on hand too, and
would do what he could to save the boy.   One of
the gentlemen looked him over, and said:

" Apparently it is going to be a matter of who
can wield the most influence with the president.   Do
you know Mr. Bliss personally?"

The Major said, with composure:

8E

" Yes; he is my uncle."

The effect was satisfactory.   There was an awk-
ward silence for a minute or more; then the
hedging and the half-confessions of over-haste and
exaggerated resentment began, and soon everything
was smooth and friendly and sociable, and it was
resolved to drop the matter and leave the boy's
bread-and-butter unmolested.

It turned out as I had expected: the president of
the road was not the Major's uncle at all — except
by adoption, and for this day and train only.

We got into no episodes on the return journey.
Probably it was because we took a night train and
slept all the way.

We left New York Saturday night by the Pennsyl-
vania road.   After breakfast the next morning we
went into the parlor-car, but found it a dull place
and dreary.   There were but few people in it and
nothing going on.   Then we went into the little
smoking-compartment of the same car and found
three gentlemen in there.   Two of them were grum-
bling over one of the rules of the road — a rule
which forbade card-playing on the trains on Sunday.
They had started an innocent game of high-low-jack
and been stopped.   The Major was interested.   He
said to the third gentleman:

" Did you object to the game?"

" Not at all.   I am a Yale professor and a religious man, but my prejudices are not extensive."

Then the Major said to the others:

" You are at perfect liberty to resume your game, gentlemen; no one here objects."

One of them declined the risk, but the other one said he would like to begin again if the Major would join him. So they spread an overcoat over their knees and the game proceeded. Pretty soon the parlor-car conductor arrived, and said brusquely:

" There, there, gentlemen, that won't do. Put up the cards— it's not allowed."

The Major was shuffling. He continued to shuffle, and said:

" By whose order is it forbidden?"

" It's my order. I forbid it."

The dealing began. The Major asked:

" Did you invent the idea?"

" What idea?"

" The idea of forbidding card-playing on Sunday."

" No — of course not."

" Who did?"

" The company."

" Then it isn't your order, after all, but the company's. Is that it?"

" Yes. But you don't stop playing; I have to require you to stop playing immediately."

" Nothing is gained by hurry, and often much is lost. Who authorized the company to issue such an order?"

" My dear sir, that is a matter of no consequence to me, and — "

" But you forget that you are not the only person concerned. It may be a matter of consequence to me. It is indeed a matter of very great importance to me. I cannot violate a legal requirement of my country without dishonoring myself; I cannot allow any man or corporation to hamper my liberties with illegal rules — a thing which railway companies are always trying to do — without dishonoring my citizenship. So I come back to that question: By whose authority has the company issued this order?''

" I don't *know*. That's *their* affair.''

" Mine, too. I doubt if the company has any right to issue such a rule. This road runs through several States. Do you know what State we are in now, and what its laws are in matters of this kind?''

" Its laws do not concern me, but the company's orders do. It is my duty to stop this game, gentlemen, and it *must* be stopped.''

" Possibly; but still there is no hurry. In hotels they post certain rules in the rooms, but they always quote passages from the State laws as authority for these requirements. I see nothing posted here of this sort. Please produce your authority and let us arrive at a decision, for you see yourself that you are marring the game.''

" I have nothing of the kind, but I have my orders, and that is sufficient. They must be obeyed.''

" Let us not jump to conclusions. It will be

better all around to examine into the matter without heat or haste, and see just where we stand before either of us makes a mistake — for the curtailing of the liberties of a citizen of the United States is a much more serious matter than you and the railroads seem to think, and it cannot be done in my person until the curtailer proves his right to do so. Now — ''

'' My dear sir, *will* you put down those cards?''

'' All in good time, perhaps. It depends. You say this order must be obeyed. *Must.* It is a strong word. You see yourself how strong it is. A wise company would not arm you with so drastic an order as this, of *course*, without appointing a penalty for its infringement. Otherwise it runs the risk of being a dead letter and a thing to laugh at. What is the appointed penalty for an infringement of this law?''

'' Penalty? I never heard of any.''

'' Unquestionably you must be mistaken. Your company orders you to come here and rudely break up an innocent amusement, and furnishes you no way to enforce the order? Don't you see that that is nonsense? What do you *do* when people refuse to obey this order? Do you take the cards away from them?''

'' No.''

'' Do you put the offender off at the next station?''

'' Well, no — of course we couldn't if he had a ticket.''

8*.*.*

" Do you have him up before a court?"

The conductor was silent and apparently troubled. The Major started a new deal, and said:

" You see that you are helpless, and that the company has placed you in a foolish position. You are furnished with an arrogant order, and you deliver it in a blustering way, and when you come to look into the matter you find you haven't any way of enforcing obedience."

The conductor said, with chill dignity:

" Gentlemen, you have heard the order, and my duty is ended. As to obeying it or not, you will do as you think fit." And he turned to leave.

" But wait. The matter is not yet finished. I think you are mistaken about your duty being ended; but if it really is, I myself have a duty to perform yet."

" How do you mean?"

" Are you going to report my disobedience at headquarters in Pittsburg?"

" No. What good would that do?"

" You must report me, or I will report you."

" Report me for what?"

" For disobeying the company's orders in not stopping this game. As a citizen it is my duty to help the railway companies keep their servants to their work."

" Are you in earnest?"

" Yes, I am in earnest. I have nothing against you as a man, but I have this against you as an officer — that you have not carried out that order, and if you do not report me I must report you. And I will.''

The conductor looked puzzled, and was thoughtful a moment; then he burst out with:

'' I seem to be getting *myself* into a scrape! It's all a muddle; I can't make head or tail of it; it's never happened before; they always knocked under and never said a word, and so *I* never saw how ridiculous that stupid order with no penalty is. *I* don't want to report anybody, and I don't want to *be* reported — why, it might do me no end of harm! Now *do* go on with the game — play the whole day if you want to — and don't let's have any more trouble about it!''

'' No, I only sat down here to establish this gentleman's rights — he can have his place now. But before you go won't you tell me what you think the company made this rule for? Can you imagine an excuse for it? I mean a rational one — an excuse that is not on its face silly, and the invention of an idiot?''

'' Why, surely I can. The reason it was made is plain enough. It is to save the feelings of the other passengers — the religious ones among them, I mean. They would not like it, to have the Sabbath desecrated by card-playing on the train.''

'' I just thought as much. They are willing to desecrate it themselves by traveling on Sunday, but they are not willing that other people — ''

H*₊*₊

" By gracious, you've hit it! I never thought of that before. The fact is, it *is* a silly rule when you come to look into it."

At this point the train-conductor arrived, and was going to shut down the game in a very high-handed fashion, but the parlor-car conductor stopped him and took him aside to explain. Nothing more was heard of the matter.

I was ill in bed eleven days in Chicago and got no glimpse of the Fair, for I was obliged to return east as soon as I was able to travel. The Major secured and paid for a state-room in a sleeper the day before we left, so that I could have plenty of room and be comfortable; but when we arrived at the station a mistake had been made and our car had not been put on. The conductor had reserved a section for us — it was the best he could do, he said. But the Major said we were not in a hurry, and would wait for the car to be put on. The conductor responded, with pleasant irony:

" It may be that *you* are not in a hurry, just as you say, but we *are*. Come, get aboard, gentlemen, get aboard — don't keep us waiting."

But the Major would not get aboard himself nor allow me to do it. He wanted his car, and said he must have it. This made the hurried and perspiring conductor impatient, and he said:

" It's the best we can *do* — we can't do impossibilities. You will take the section or go without. A mistake has been made and can't be rectified at

this late hour.   It's a thing that happens now and
then, and there is nothing for it but to put up with
it and make the best of it.   Other people do.''

" Ah, that is just it, you see.   If they had stuck
to their rights and enforced them you wouldn't be
trying to trample mine under foot in this bland way
now.   I haven't any disposition to give you un-
necessary trouble, but it is my duty to protect the
next man from this kind of imposition.   So I must
have my car.   Otherwise I will wait in Chicago and
sue the company for violating its contract.''

" Sue the company? — for a thing like that!''

" Certainly.''

" Do you really mean that?''

" Indeed, I do.''

The conductor looked the Major over wonder-
ingly, and then said:

" It beats me — it's bran-new — I've never struck
the mate to it before.   But I swear I think you'd
do it.   Look here, I'll send for the station-master.''

When the station-master came he was a good deal
annoyed — at the Major, not at the person who had
made the mistake.   He was rather brusque, and
took the same position which the conductor had
taken in the beginning; but he failed to move the
soft-spoken artilleryman, who still insisted that he
must have his car.   However, it was plain that there
was only one strong side in this case, and that that
side was the Major's.   The station-master banished
his annoyed manner, and became pleasant and even

PRIVATE HISTORY OF THE "JUMPING FROG" STORY

FIVE or six years ago a lady from Finland asked me to tell her a story in our negro dialect, so that she could get an idea of what that variety of speech was like. I told her one of Hopkinson Smith's negro stories, and gave her a copy of *Harper's Monthly* containing it. She translated it for a Swedish newspaper, but by an oversight named me as the author of it instead of Smith. I was very sorry for that, because I got a good lashing in the Swedish press, which would have fallen to his share but for that mistake; for it was shown that Boccaccio had told that very story, in his curt and meagre fashion, five hundred years before Smith took hold of it and made a good and tellable thing out of it.

I have always been sorry for Smith. But my own turn has come now. A few weeks ago Professor Van Dyke, of Princeton, asked this question:

" Do you know how old your Jumping Frog story is?"

And I answered:

"Yes — forty-five years.   The thing happened in Calaveras County in the spring of 1849."

"No; it happened earlier — a couple of thousand years earlier; it is a Greek story."

I was astonished — and hurt.   I said:

"I am willing to be a literary thief if it has been so ordained; I am even willing to be caught robbing the ancient dead alongside of Hopkinson Smith, for he is my friend and a good fellow, and I think would be as honest as any one if he could do it without occasioning remark; but I am not willing to ante-date his crimes by fifteen hundred years.   I must ask you to knock off part of that."

But the professor was not chaffing; he was in earnest, and could not abate a century.   He named the Greek author, and offered to get the book and send it to me and the college text-book containing the English translation also.   I thought I would like the translation best, because Greek makes me tired. January 30th he sent me the English version, and I will presently insert it in this article.   It is my Jumping Frog tale in every essential.   It is not strung out as I have strung it out, but it is all there.

To me this is very curious and interesting. Curious for several reasons.   For instance:

I heard the story told by a man who was not telling it to his hearers as a thing new to them, but as a thing which *they had witnessed and would remember*.   He was a dull person, and ignorant; he

and learn that frog to jump. And you bet you he *did* learn him, too.
He'd give him a little punch behind, and the next minute you'd see
that frog whirling in the air like a doughnut — see him turn one summer-
set, or maybe a couple if he got a good start, and come down flat-footed
and all right, like a cat. He got him up so in the matter of ketching
flies, and kep' him in practice so constant, that he'd nail a fly every time
as fur as he could see him. Smiley said all a frog wanted was education, and he could do 'most anything — and I believe him. Why, I've
seen him set Dan'l Webster down here on this floor — Dan'l Webster
was the name of the frog — and sing out " Flies, Dan'l, flies ! " and
quicker'n you could wink he'd spring straight up and snake a fly off'n
the counter there, and flop down on the floor ag'in as solid as a gob of
mud, and fall to scratching the side of his head with his hind foot as
indifferent as if he hadn't no idea he'd been doin' any more'n any frog
might do. You never see a frog so modest and straightfor'ard as he
was, for all he was so gifted. And when it come to fair and square
jumping on a dead level, he could get over more ground at one straddle
than any animal of his breed you ever see. Jumping on a dead level
was his strong suit, you understand; and when it came to that, Smiley
would ante up money on him as long as he had a red. Smiley was
monstrous proud of his frog, and well he might be, for fellers that had
traveled and been everywheres all said he laid over any frog that ever
they see.

Well, Smiley kep' the beast in a little lattice box, and he used to
fetch him down-town sometimes and lay for a bet. One day a feller
— a stranger in the camp, he was — come acrost him with his box,
and says:

" What might it be that you've got in the box? "

And Smiley says, sorter indifferent-like, " It might be a parrot, or it
might be a canary, maybe, but it ain't — it's only just a frog."

And the feller took it, and looked at it careful, and turned it round this
way and that, and says, " H'm — so 'tis. Well, what's *he* good for? "

" Well," Smiley says, easy and careless, " he's good enough for *one*
thing, I should judge — he can outjump any frog in Calaveras County."

The feller took the box again and took another long, particular look,
and gave it back to Smiley, and says, very deliberate, " Well," he says,
" I don't see no p'ints about that frog that's any better'n any other
frog."

" Maybe you don't," Smiley says. " Maybe you understand frogs and maybe you don't understand 'em; maybe you've had experience, and maybe you ain't only a amature, as it were. Anyways, I've got *my* opinion, and I'll resk forty dollars that he can outjump any frog in Calaveras County."

And the feller studies a minute, and then says, kinder sad-like, "Well, I'm only a stranger here, and I ain't got no frog, but if I had a frog I'd bet you."

And then Smiley says: "That's all right — that's all right — if you'll hold my box a minute, I'll go and get you a frog." And so the feller took the box and put up his forty dollars along with Smiley's and set down to wait.

So he set there a good while thinking and thinking to hisself, and then he got the frog out and prized his mouth open and took a teaspoon and filled him full of quail shot — filled him pretty near up to his chin — and set him on the floor. Smiley he went to the swamp and slopped around in the mud for a long time, and finally he ketched a frog and fetched him in and give him to this feller, and says:

"Now, if you're ready, set him alongside of Dan'l, with his fore-paws just even with Dan'l's, and I'll give the word." Then he says, "One — two — three — *git!*" and him and the feller touched up the frogs from behind, and the new frog hopped off lively; but Dan'l give a heave, and hysted up his shoulders — so — like a Frenchman, but it warn't no use — he couldn't budge; he was planted as solid as a church, and he couldn't no more stir than if he was anchored out. Smiley was a good deal surprised, and he was disgusted, too, but he didn't have no idea what the matter was, of course.

The feller took the money and started away; and when he was going out at the door he sorter jerked his thumb over his shoulder — so — at Dan'l, and says again, very deliberate: "Well," he says, "*I* don't see no p'ints about that frog that's any better'n any other frog."

Smiley he stood scratching his head and looking down at Dan'l a long time, and at last he says, "I do wonder what in the nation that frog throw'd off for — I wonder if there ain't something the matter with him — he 'pears to look mighty baggy, somehow." And he ketched Dan'l by the nap of the neck, and hefted him, and says, "Why, blame my cats if he don't weigh five pound!" and turned him upside down, and he belched out a double handful of shot. And then he see how it was, and he was the maddest man — he set the frog down and took out after that feller, but he never ketched him.

9ᴱ

The resemblances are deliciously exact. There you have the wily Bœotian and the wily Jim Smiley waiting — two thousand years apart — and waiting, each equipped with his frog and " laying " for the stranger. A contest is proposed — for money. The Athenian would take a chance " if the other would fetch him a frog "; the Yankee says: " I'm only a stranger here, and I ain't got no frog; but if I had a frog I'd bet you." The wily Bœotian and the wily Californian, with that vast gulf of two thousand years between, retire eagerly and go frogging in the marsh; the Athenian and the Yankee remain behind and work a base advantage, the one with pebbles, the other with shot. Presently the contest began. In the one case " they pinched the Bœotian frog "; in the other, " him and the feller touched up the frogs from behind." The Bœotian frog " gathered himself for a leap " (you can just *see* him!), " but could not move his body in the least ": the Californian frog " give a heave, but it warn't no use — he couldn't budge." In both the ancient and the modern cases the strangers departed with the money. The Bœotian and the Californian wonder what is the matter with their frogs; they lift them and examine; they turn them upside down and out spills the informing ballast.

Yes, the resemblances are curiously exact. I used to tell the story of the Jumping Frog in San Francisco, and presently Artemus Ward came along and wanted it to help fill out a little book which he was about to publish; so I wrote it out and sent it to his publisher, Carleton; but Carleton thought the book had enough matter in it, so he gave the story to Henry Clapp as a present, and Clapp put it in his *Saturday Press*, and it killed that paper with a suddenness that was beyond praise. At least the paper died with that issue, and none but envious people have ever tried to rob me of the honor and credit of killing it. The "Jumping Frog" was the first piece of writing of mine that spread itself through the newspapers and brought me into public notice. Consequently, the *Saturday Press* was a cocoon and I the worm in it; also, I was the gay-colored literary moth which its death set free. This simile has been used before.

Early in '66 the "Jumping Frog" was issued in book form, with other sketches of mine. A year or two later Madame Blanc translated it into French and published it in the *Revue des Deux Mondes*, but the result was not what should have been expected, for the *Revue* struggled along and pulled through, and is alive yet. I think the fault must have been in the translation. I ought to have translated it myself. I think so because I examined into the matter and finally retranslated the sketch from the French back into English, to see what the trouble was; that is, to see just what sort of a focus the French people got upon it. Then the mystery was explained. In French the story is too confused, and chaotic, and unreposeful, and ungrammatical, and insane; consequently it could only cause grief and sickness — it could not kill. A glance at my re-translation will show the reader that this must be true.

[*My Re-translation.*]

THE FROG JUMPING OF THE COUNTY OF CALAVERAS.

Eh bien! this Smiley nourished some terriers à rats, and some cocks of combat, and some cats, and all sort of things; and with his rage of betting one no had more of repose. He trapped one day a frog and him imported with him (et l'emporta chez lui) saying that he pretended to make his education. You me believe if you will, but during three months he not has nothing done but to him apprehend to jump (apprendre à sauter) in a court retired of her mansion (de sa maison). And I you respond that he have succeeded. He him gives a small blow by behind, and the instant after you shall see the frog turn in the air like a grease-biscuit, make one summersault, sometimes two, when she was well started, and re-fall upon his feet like a cat. He him had accomplished in the art of to gobble the flies (gober des mouches), and him there exercised continually — so well that a fly at the most far that she appeared was a fly lost. Smiley had custom to say that all which lacked to a frog it was the education, but with the education she could do nearly all — and I him believe. Tenez, I him have seen pose Daniel Webster there upon this plank — Daniel Webster was the name of the frog — and to him sing, "Some flies, Daniel, some flies!" — in a flash of the eye Daniel had bounded and seized a fly here upon the counter, then jumped anew at the earth, where he rested truly to himself scratch the head with his behind-foot, as if he no had not the least idea of his superiority. Never you not have seen frog as modest, as natural, sweet as she was. And when he himself agitated to jump purely and simply upon plain earth, she does more ground in one jump than any beast of his species than you can know.

To jump plain — this was his strong. When he himself agitated for that Smiley multiplied the bets upon her as long as there to him remained a red. It must to know, Smiley was monstrously proud of his frog, and he of it was right, for some men who were traveled, who had all seen, said that they to him would be injurious to him compare to another frog. Smiley guarded Daniel in a little box latticed which he carried bytimes to the village for some bet.

One day an individual stranger at the camp him arrested with his box and him said:

"What is this that you have then shut up there within?"

Smiley said, with an air indifferent:

"That could be a paroquet, or a syringe (*ou un serin*), but this no is nothing of such, it not is but a frog."

The individual it took, it regarded with care, it turned from one side and from the other, then he said:

"*Tiens!* in effect! — At what is she good?"

"My God!" respond Smiley, always with an air disengaged, "she is good for one thing, to my notice (*à mon avis*), she can batter in jumping (*elle peut batter en sautant*) all frogs of the county of Calaveras."

The individual re-took the box, it examined of new longly, and it rendered to Smiley in saying with an air deliberate:

"*Eh bien!* I no saw not that that frog had nothing of better than each frog." (*Je ne vois pas que cette grenouille ait rien de mieux qu'aucune grenouille.*) [If that isn't grammar gone to seed, then I count myself no judge. — M. T.]

"Possible that you not it saw not," said Smiley, "possible that you —you comprehend frogs; possible that you not you there comprehend nothing; possible that you had of the experience, and possible that you not be but an amateur. Of all manner (*De toute manière*) I bet forty dollars that she batter in jumping no matter which frog of the county of Calaveras."

The individual reflected a second, and said like sad:

"I not am but a stranger here, I no have not a frog; but if I of it had one, I would embrace the bet."

"Strong, well!" respond Smiley; "nothing of more facility. If you will hold my box a minute, I go you to search a frog (*j'irai vous chercher*)."

Behold, then, the individual, who guards the box, who puts his forty dollars upon those of Smiley, and who attends (*et qui attend*). He attended enough longtimes, reflecting all solely. And figure you that he takes Daniel, him opens the mouth by force and with a teaspoon him fills with shot of the hunt, even him fills just to the chin, then he him puts by the earth. Smiley during these times was at slopping in a swamp. Finally he trapped (*attrape*) a frog, him carried to that individual, and said:

"Now if you be ready, put him all against Daniel, with their before-
9*₊*₊

feet upon the same line, and I give the signal"—then he added:
"One, two, three—advance!"

Him and the individual touched their frogs by behind, and the frog
new put to jump smartly, but Daniel himself lifted ponderously, exalted
the shoulders thus, like a Frenchman—to what good? he could not
budge, he is planted solid like a church, he not advance no more than if
one him had put at the anchor.

Smiley was surprised and disgusted, but he not himself doubted not
of the turn being intended (*mais il ne se doutait pas du tour bien
entendu*). The individual empocketed the silver, himself with it went,
and of it himself in going is that he no gives not a jerk of thumb over
the shoulder—like that—at the poor Daniel, in saying with his air
deliberate—(*L'individu empoche l'argent s'en va et en s'en allant est
ce qu'il ne donne pas un coup de pouce par-dessus l'épaule, comme, ça,
au pauvre Daniel, en disant de son air délibéré.*)

"Eh bien!   *I no see not that that frog has nothing of better than
another*."

Smiley himself scratched longtimes the head, the eyes fixed upon
Daniel, until that which at last he said:

"I me demand how the devil it makes itself that this beast has refused.
Is it that she had something?   One would believe that she is stuffed."

He grasped Daniel by the skin of the neck, him lifted and said:

"The wolf me bite if he no weigh not five pounds."

He him reversed and the unhappy belched two handfuls of shot
(*et le malheureux*, etc.).—When Smiley recognized how it was, he
was like mad.   He deposited his frog by the earth and ran after that
individual, but he not him caught never.

It may be that there are people who can translate
better than I can, but I am not acquainted with them.

So ends the private and public history of the
Jumping Frog of Calaveras County, an incident
which has this unique feature about it — that it is
both old and new, a " chestnut " and not a " chestnut "; for it was original when it happened two
thousand years ago, and was again original when it
happened in California in our own time.

MENTAL TELEGRAPHY AGAIN

I HAVE three or four curious incidents to tell about. They seem to come under the head of what I named " Mental Telegraphy " in a paper written seventeen years ago, and published long afterwards.*

Several years ago I made a campaign on the platform with Mr. George W. Cable. In Montreal we were honored with a reception. It began at two in the afternoon in a long drawing-room in the Windsor Hotel. Mr. Cable and I stood at one end of this room, and the ladies and gentlemen entered it at the other end, crossed it at that end, then came up the long left-hand side, shook hands with us, said a word or two, and passed on, in the usual way. My sight is of the telescopic sort, and I presently recognized a familiar face among the throng of strangers drifting in at the distant door, and I said to myself, with surprise and high gratification, " That is Mrs. R.; I had forgotten that she was a Canadian." She had been a great friend of mine in Carson City, Nevada, in the early days. I had not seen her or

---

*The paper entitled " Mental Telegraphy," which originally appeared in *Harper's Magazine* for December, 1893, is included in the volume entitled *The American Claimant and Other Stories and Sketches.*

I*₊*₊

heard of her for twenty years; I had not been
thinking about her; there was nothing to suggest
her to me, nothing to bring her to my mind; in
fact, to me she had long ago ceased to exist, and
had disappeared from my consciousness. But I
knew her instantly; and I saw her so clearly that I
was able to note some of the particulars of her dress,
and did note them, and they remained in my mind.
I was impatient for her to come. In the midst of
the hand-shakings I snatched glimpses of her and
noted her progress with the slow-moving file across
the end of the room; then I saw her start up the
side, and this gave me a full front view of her face.
I saw her last when she was within twenty-five feet
of me. For an hour I kept thinking she must still
be in the room somewhere and would come at last,
but I was disappointed.

When I arrived in the lecture-hall that evening
some one said: "Come into the waiting-room;
there's a friend of yours there who wants to see
you. You'll not be introduced — you are to do the
recognizing without help if you can."

I said to myself: "It is Mrs. R.; I shan't have
any trouble."

There were perhaps ten ladies present, all seated.
In the midst of them was Mrs. R., as I had expected. She was dressed exactly as she was when I
had seen her in the afternoon. I went forward and
shook hands with her and called her by name, and
said:

"I knew you the moment you appeared at the reception this afternoon."

She looked surprised, and said: "But I was not at the reception. I have just arrived from Quebec, and have not been in town an hour."

It was my turn to be surprised now. I said: "I can't help it. I give you my word of honor that it is as I say. I saw you at the reception, and you were dressed precisely as you are now. When they told me a moment ago that I should find a friend in this room, your image rose before me, dress and all, just as I had seen you at the reception."

Those are the facts. She was not at the reception at all, or anywhere near it; but I saw her there nevertheless, and most clearly and unmistakably. To that I could make oath. How is one to explain this? I was not thinking of her at the time; had not thought of her for years. But she had been thinking of me, no doubt; did her thoughts flit through leagues of air to me, and bring with it that clear and pleasant vision of herself? I think so. That was and remains my sole experience in the matter of apparitions — I mean apparitions that come when one is (ostensibly) awake. I could have been asleep for a moment; the apparition could have been the creature of a dream. Still, that is nothing to the point; the feature of interest is the happening of the thing just at that time, instead of at an earlier or later time, which is argument that its origin lay in thought-transference.

on-the-Hudson with Mr. John Brisben Walker, of
the *Cosmopolitan* magazine. We came into New
York next morning, and went to the Century Club
for luncheon. He said some praiseful things about
the character of the club and the orderly serenity and
pleasantness of its quarters, and asked if I had never
tried to acquire membership in it. I said I had not,
and that New York clubs were a continuous expense
to the country members without being of frequent
use or benefit to them.

"And now I've got an idea!" said I. "There's
the Lotos — the first New York club I was ever a
member of · — my very earliest love in that line. I
have been a member of it for considerably more
than twenty years, yet have seldom had a chance to
look in and see the boys. They turn gray and grow
old while I am not watching. And *my dues go on*.
I am going to Hartford this afternoon for a day or
two, but as soon as I get back I will go to John
Elderkin very privately and say: ' Remember the
veteran and confer distinction upon him, for the
sake of old times. Make me an honorary member
and abolish the tax. If you haven't any such thing
as honorary membership, all the better — create it
for my honor and glory.' That would be a great
thing; I will go to John Elderkin as soon as I get
back from Hartford."

I took the last express that afternoon, first tele-
graphing Mr. F. G. Whitmore to come and see me
next day. When he came he asked:

" Did you get a letter from Mr. John Elderkin, secretary of the Lotos Club, before you left New York?"

" No."

" Then it just missed you.   If I had known you were coming I would have kept it.   It is beautiful, and will make you proud.   The Board of Directors, by unanimous vote, have made you a life member, and *squelched those dues;* and, you are to be on hand and receive your distinction on the night of the 30th, which is the twenty-fifth anniversary of the founding of the club, and it will not surprise me if they have some great times there."

What put the honorary membership in my head that day in the Century Club? for I had never thought of it before.   I don't know what brought the thought to me at *that* particular time instead of earlier, but I am well satisfied that it originated with the Board of Directors, and had been on its way to my brain through the air ever since the moment that saw their vote recorded.

Another incident.   I was in Hartford two or three days as a guest of the Rev. Joseph H. Twichell.   I have held the rank of Honorary Uncle to his children for a quarter of a century, and I went out with him in the trolley-car to visit one of my nieces, who is at Miss Porter's famous school in Farmington. The distance is eight or nine miles.   On the way, talking, I illustrated something with an anecdote. This is the anecdote:

" Here we are at Farmington," said Twichell, interrupting.

We left the trolley-car and tramped through the mud a hundred yards or so to the school, talking about the time we and Warner walked out there years ago, and the pleasant time we had.

We had a visit with my niece in the parlor, then started for the trolley again.   Outside the house we encountered a double rank of twenty or thirty of Miss Porter's young ladies arriving from a walk, and we stood aside, ostensibly to let them have room to file past, but really to look at them.   Presently one of them stepped out of the rank and said:

" You don't know me, Mr. Twichell, but I know your daughter, and that gives me the privilege of shaking hands with you."

Then she put out her hand to me, and said:

" And I wish to shake hands with you too, Mr. Clemens.   You don't remember me, but you were introduced to me in the arcade in Milan two years and a half ago by Lieutenant H."

What had put that story into my head after all that stretch of time?   Was it just the proximity of that young girl, or was it merely an odd accident?

WHAT PAUL BOURGET THINKS OF US

HE reports the American joke correctly. In Boston they ask, How much does he know? in New York, How much is he worth? in Philadelphia, Who were his parents? And when an alien observer turns his telescope upon us — advertisedly in our own special interest — a natural apprehension moves us to ask, What is the diameter of his reflector?

I take a great interest in M. Bourget's chapters, for I know by the newspapers that there are several Americans who are expecting to get a whole education out of them; several who foresaw, and also foretold, that our long night was over, and a light almost divine about to break upon the land.

"His utterances concerning us are bound to be weighty and well timed."

"He gives us an object-lesson which should be thoughtfully and profitably studied."

These well-considered and important verdicts were of a nature to restore public confidence, which had been disquieted by questionings as to whether so young a teacher would be qualified to take so large a class as 70,000,000, distributed over so extensive a schoolhouse as America, and pull it through without assistance.

I was even disquieted myself, although I am of a cold, calm temperament, and not easily disturbed. I feared for my country. And I was not wholly tranquilized by the verdicts rendered as above. It seemed to me that there was still room for doubt. In fact, in looking the ground over I became more disturbed than I was before. Many worrying questions came up in my mind. Two were prominent. Where had the teacher gotten his equipment? What was his method?

He had gotten his equipment in France.

Then as to his method! I saw by his own intimations that he was an Observer, and had a System — that used by naturalists and other scientists. The naturalist collects many bugs and reptiles and butterflies and studies their ways a long time patiently. By this means he is presently able to group these creatures into families and subdivisions of families by nice shadings of differences observable in their characters. Then he labels all those shaded bugs and things with nicely descriptive group names, and is now happy, for his great work is completed, and as a result he intimately knows every bug and shade of a bug there, inside and out. It may be true, but a person who was not a naturalist would feel safer about it if he had the opinion of the bug. I think it is a pleasant System, but subject to error.

The Observer of Peoples has to be a Classifier, a

Grouper, a Deducer, a Generalizer, a Psychologizer;
and, first and last, a Thinker. He has to be all
these, and when he is at home, observing his own
folk, he is often able to prove competency. But history has shown that when he is abroad observing
unfamiliar peoples the chances are heavily against
him. He is then a naturalist observing a bug, with
no more than a naturalist's chance of being able
to tell the bug anything new about itself, and
no more than a naturalist's chance of being able
to teach it any new ways which it will prefer to its
own.

To return to that first question. M. Bourget, as
teacher, would simply be France teaching America.
It seemed to me that the outlook was dark — almost
Egyptian, in fact. What would the new teacher,
representing France, teach us? Railroading? No.
France knows nothing valuable about railroading.
Steamshipping? No. France has no superiorities
over us in that matter. Steamboating? No. French
steamboating is still of Fulton's date — 1809. Postal
service? No. France is a back number there.
Telegraphy? No, we taught her that ourselves.
Journalism? No. Magazining? No, that is our
own specialty. Government? No; Liberty, Equal-
ity, Fraternity, Nobility, Democracy, Adultery —
the system is too variegated for our climate.
Religion? No, not variegated enough for our
climate. Morals? No, we cannot rob the poor to
enrich ourselves. Novel-writing? No. M. Bour-

get and the others know only one plan, and when
that is expurgated there is nothing left of the book.

I wish I could think what he is going to teach us.
Can it be Deportment? But he experimented in that
at Newport and failed to give satisfaction, except to
a few. Those few are pleased. They are enjoying
their joy as well as they can. They confess their
happiness to the interviewer. They feel pretty
striped, but they remember with reverent recognition that they had sugar between the cuts. True,
sugar with sand in it, but sugar. And true, they
had some trouble to tell which was sugar and which
was sand, because the sugar itself looked just like the
sand, and also had a gravelly taste; still, they knew
that the sugar was there, and would have been very
good sugar indeed if it had been screened. Yes,
they are pleased; not noisily so, but pleased; in-
vaded, or streaked, as one may say, with little re-
current shivers of joy — subdued joy, so to speak,
not the overdone kind. And they commune together, these, and massage each other with comfort-
ing sayings, in a sweet spirit of resignation and
thankfulness, mixing these elements in the same
proportions as the sugar and the sand, as a memo-
rial, and saying, the one to the other, and to the
interviewer: " It was severe — yes, it was bitterly
severe; but oh, how true it was; and it will do us
so much good!"

If it isn't Deportment, what is left? It was at
this point that I seemed to get on the right track at

last. M. Bourget would teach us to know ourselves; that was it: he would reveal us to ourselves. That would be an education. He would explain us to ourselves. Then we should understand ourselves; and after that be able to go on more intelligently.

It seemed a doubtful scheme. He could explain *us* to *him*self — that would be easy. That would be the same as the naturalist explaining the bug to himself. But to explain the bug to the bug — that is quite a different matter. The bug may not know himself perfectly, but he knows himself better than the naturalist can know him, at any rate.

A foreigner can photograph the exteriors of a nation, but I think that that is as far as he can get. I think that no foreigner can report its interior — its soul, its life, its speech, its thought. I think that a knowledge of these things is acquirable in only one way; not two or four or six—*absorption ;* years and years of unconscious absorption; years and years of intercourse with the life concerned; of living it, indeed; sharing personally in its shames and prides, its joys and griefs, its loves and hates, its pros-perities and reverses, its shows and shabbinesses, its deep patriotisms, its whirlwinds of political pas-sion, its adorations — of flag, and heroic dead, and the glory of the national name. Observation? Of what real value is it? One learns peoples through the heart, not the eyes or the intellect.

There is only one expert who is qualified to ex-amine the souls and the life of a people and make a

10*₊*₊

valuable report — the native novelist. This expert is
so rare that the most populous country can never
have fifteen conspicuously and confessedly competent
ones in stock at one time. This native specialist is
not qualified to begin work until he has been absorb-
ing during twenty-five years. How much of his
competency is derived from conscious " observation"? The amount is so slight that it counts for
next to nothing in the equipment. Almost the
whole capital of the novelist is the slow accumula-
tion of *un*conscious observation — absorption. The
native expert's intentional observation of manners,
speech, character, and ways of life can have value,
for the native knows what they mean without having
to cipher out the meaning. But I should be astonished to see a foreigner get at the right meanings,
catch the elusive shades of these subtle things.
Even the native novelist becomes a foreigner, with a
foreigner's limitations, when he steps from the State
whose life is familiar to him into a State whose life
he has not lived. Bret Harte got his California and
his Californians by unconscious absorption, and put
both of them into his tales alive. But when he
came from the Pacific to the Atlantic and tried to
do Newport life from study — conscious observation — his failure was absolutely monumental.
Newport is a disastrous place for the unacclimated
observer, evidently.

To return to novel-building. Does the native
novelist try to generalize the nation? No, he lays

plainly before you the ways and speech and life of a few people grouped in a certain place — his own place — and that is one book.   In time he and his brethren will report to you the life and the people of the whole nation — the life of a group in a New England village; in a New York village; in a Texan village; in an Oregon village; in villages in fifty States and Territories; then the farm-life in fifty States and Territories; a hundred patches of life and groups of people in a dozen widely separated cities.   And the Indians will be attended to; and the cowboys; and the gold and silver miners; and the negroes; and the Idiots and Congressmen; and the Irish, the Germans, the Italians, the Swedes, the French, the Chinamen, the Greasers; and the Catholics, the Methodists, the Presbyterians, the Congregationalists, the Baptists, the Spiritualists, the Mormons, the Shakers, the Quakers, the Jews, the Campbellites, the infidels, the Christian Scientists, the Mind-Curists, the Faith-Curists, the train-robbers, the White Caps, the Moonshiners.   And when a thousand able novels have been written, *there* you have the soul of the people, the life of the people, the speech of the people; and not any-where else can these be had.   And the shadings of character, manners, feelings, ambitions, will be infinite.

" *The nature of a people* is always of a similar shade in its vices and its virtues, in its frivolities and in its labor. *It is this physiognomy which it is necessary to discover*, and every document is good, from the

J*.*.

hall of a casino to the church, from the foibles of a fashionable woman
to the suggestions of a revolutionary leader. I am therefore quite sure
that this *American soul*, the principal interest and the great object of
my voyage, appears behind the records of Newport for those who choose
to see it." — *M. Paul Bourget.*

[The italics are mine.] It is a large contract
which he has undertaken. " Records " is a pretty
poor word there, but I think the use of it is due to
hasty translation. In the original the word is *fastes*.
I think M. Bourget meant to suggest that he expected to find the great " American soul " secreted
behind the *ostentations* of Newport; and that he
was going to get it out and examine it, and generalize it, and psychologize it, and make it reveal to
him its hidden vast mystery: " the nature of the
people " of the United States of America. We
have been accused of being a nation addicted to
inventing wild schemes. I trust that we shall be
allowed to retire to second place now.

There isn't a single human characteristic that can
be safely labeled " American." There isn't a single
human ambition, or religious trend, or drift of
thought, or peculiarity of education, or code of
principles, or breed of folly, or style of conversation, or preference for a particular subject for discussion, or form of legs or trunk or head or face or
expression or complexion, or gait, or dress, or
manners, or disposition, or any other human detail,
inside or outside, that can rationally be generalized
as " American."

Whenever you have found what seems to be an

" American " peculiarity, you have only to cross a
frontier or two, or go down or up in the social scale,
and you perceive that it has disappeared.   And you
can cross the Atlantic and find it again.   There
may be a Newport religious drift, or sporting drift,
or conversational style or complexion, or cut of
face, but there are entire empires in America, north,
south, east, and west, where you could not find
your duplicates.   It is the same with everything
else which one might propose to call " American."
M. Bourget thinks he has found the American
Coquette.   If he had really found her he would also
have found, I am sure, that she was not new, that
she exists in other lands in the same forms, and
with the same frivolous heart and the same ways
and impulses.   I think this because I have seen our
coquette; I have seen her in life; better still, I have
seen her in our novels, and seen her twin in foreign
novels.   I wish M. Bourget had seen ours.   He
thought he saw her.   And so he applied his System
to her.   She was a Species.   So he gathered a
number of samples of what seemed to be her, and
put them under his glass, and divided them into
groups which he calls " types," and labeled them in
his usual scientific way with " formulas " — brief
sharp descriptive flashes that make a person blink,
sometimes, they are so sudden and vivid.   As a
rule they are pretty far-fetched, but that is not an
important matter; they surprise, they compel admiration, and I notice by some of the comments

conspiracy to freight him up with all the strange extravagances those people's decayed brains could invent.

The lengths to which they went are next to incredible. They told him things which surely would have excited any one else's suspicion, but they did not excite his. Consider this:

" There is not in all the United States an entirely nude statue."

If an angel should come down and say such a thing about heaven, a reasonably cautious observer would take that angel's number and inquire a little further before he added it to his catch. What does the present observer do? Adds it. Adds it at once. Adds it, and labels it with this innocent comment:

"This small fact is strangely significant."

It does seem to me that this kind of observing is defective.

Here is another curiosity which some liberal person made him a present of. I should think it ought to have disturbed the deep slumber of his suspicion a little, but it didn't. It was a note from a fog-horn for strenuousness, it seems to me, but the doomed voyager did not catch it. If he had but caught it, it would have saved him from several disasters:

" If the American knows that you are traveling to take notes, he is interested in it, and at the same time rejoices in it, as in a tribute."

Again, this is defective observation. It is human to like to be praised; one can even notice it in the

French.   But it is not human to like to be ridiculed, even when it comes in the form of a " tribute."   I think a little psychologizing ought to have come in there.   Something like this: A dog does not like to be ridiculed, a redskin does not like to be ridiculed, a negro does not like to be ridiculed, a Chinaman does not like to be ridiculed; let us deduce from these significant facts this formula: the American's grade being higher than these, and the chain of argument stretching unbroken all the way up to him, there is room for suspicion that the person who said the American likes to be ridiculed, and regards it as a tribute, is not a capable observer.

I feel persuaded that in the matter of psychologizing, a professional is too apt to yield to the fascinations of the loftier regions of that great art, to the neglect of its lowlier walks.   Every now and then, at half-hour intervals, M. Bourget collects a hatful of airy inaccuracies and dissolves them in a panful of assorted abstractions, and runs the charge into a mould and turns you out a compact principle which will explain an American girl, or an American woman, or why new people yearn for old things, or any other impossible riddle which a person wants answered.

It seems to be conceded that there are a few human peculiarities that can be generalized and located here and there in the world and named by the name of the nation where they are found.   I wonder what they are.   Perhaps one of them is

money is " American " ; and that the mad desire to
get suddenly rich is " American." I believe that
both of these things are merely and broadly human,
not American monopolies at all. The love of money
is natural to all nations, for money is a good and
strong friend. I think that this love has existed
everywhere, ever since the Bible called it the root of
all evil.

I think that the reason why we Americans seem
to be so addicted to trying to get rich suddenly is
merely because the *opportunity* to make promising
efforts in that direction has offered itself to us with
a frequency out of all proportion to the European
experience. For eighty years this opportunity has
been offering itself in one new town or region after
another straight westward, step by step, all the way
from the Atlantic coast to the Pacific. When a
mechanic could buy ten town lots on tolerably long
credit for ten months' savings out of his wages, and
reasonably expect to sell them in a couple of years
for ten times what he gave for them, it was human
for him to try the venture, and he did it no matter
what his nationality was. He would have done it in
Europe or China if he had had the same chance.

In the flush times in the silver regions a cook or
any other humble worker stood a very good chance
to get rich out of a trifle of money risked in a stock
deal; and that person promptly took that risk, no
matter what his or her nationality might be. I was
there, and saw it.

But these opportunities have not been plenty in our Southern States; so there you have a prodigious region where the rush for sudden wealth is almost an unknown thing — and has been, from the beginning.

Europe has offered few opportunities for poor Tom, Dick, and Harry; but when she has offered one, there has been no noticeable difference between European eagerness and American. England saw this in the wild days of the Railroad King; France saw it in 1720 — time of Law and the Mississippi Bubble. I am sure I have never seen in the gold and silver mines any madness, fury, frenzy to get suddenly rich which was even remotely comparable to that which raged in France in the Bubble day. If I had a cyclopædia here I could turn to that memorable case, and satisfy nearly anybody that the hunger for the sudden dollar is no more " American " than it is French. And if I could furnish an American opportunity to staid Germany, I think I could wake her up like a house afire.

But I must return to the Generalizations, Psychologizings, Deductions. When M. Bourget is exploiting these arts, it is then that he is peculiarly and particularly himself. His ways are wholly original when he encounters a trait or a custom which is new to him. Another person would merely examine the find, verify it, estimate its value, and let it go; but that is not sufficient for M. Bourget: he always wants to know *why* that thing exists, he wants to know how it came to happen; and he will not let go

11E

of it until he has found out.   And in every instance
he will find that reason where no one but himself
would have thought of looking for it.   He does not
seem to care for a reason that is not picturesquely
located; one might almost say picturesquely and
impossibly located.

He found out that in America men do not try to
hunt down young married women.   At once, as
usual, he wanted to know *why*.   Any one could
have told him.   He could have divined it by the
lights thrown by the novels of the country.   But
no, he preferred to find out for himself.   He has a
trustfulness as regards men and facts which is fine
and unusual; he is not particular about the source
of a fact, he is not particular about the character
and standing of the fact itself; but when it comes to
pounding out the reason for the existence of the
fact, he will trust no one but himself.

In the present instance here was his fact: American young married women are not pursued by the
corruptor; and here was the question: What is it
that protects her?

It seems quite unlikely that that problem could
have offered difficulties to any but a trained philoso-
pher.   Nearly any person would have said to M.
Bourget: " Oh, that is very simple.   It is very
seldom in America that a marriage is made on a
commercial basis; our marriages, from the beginning, have been made for love; and where love is
there is no room for the corruptor."

Now, it is interesting to see the formidable way in which M. Bourget went at that poor, humble little thing. He moved upon it in column — three columns — and with artillery.

" Two reasons of a very different kind explain " — that fact.

And now that I have got so far, I am almost afraid to say what his two reasons are, lest I be charged with inventing them. But I will not retreat now; I will condense them and print them, giving my word that I am honest and not trying to deceive any one.

1. Young married women are protected from the approaches of the seducer in New England and vicinity by the diluted remains of a prudence created by a Puritan law of two hundred years ago, which for a while punished adultery with death.

2. And young married women of the other forty or fifty States are protected by laws which afford extraordinary facilities for divorce.

If I have not lost my mind I have accurately conveyed those two Vesuvian irruptions of philosophy. But the reader can consult Chapter IV. of *Outre-Mer*, and decide for himself. Let us examine this paralyzing Deduction or Explanation by the light of a few sane facts.

1. This universality of " protection " has existed in our country *from the beginning ;* before the death penalty existed in New England, and during all the generations that have dragged by since it was annulled.

2. Extraordinary facilities for divorce are of such
recent creation that any middle-aged American can
remember a time when such things had not yet been
thought of.

Let us suppose that the first easy divorce law
went into effect forty years ago, and got noised
around and fairly started in business thirty-five years
ago, when we had, say, 25,000,000 of white population. Let us suppose that among 5,000,000 of
them the young married women were " protected "
by the surviving shudder of that ancient Puritan
scare — what is M. Bourget going to do about those
who lived among the 20,000,000? They were clean
in their morals, they were pure, yet there was no
easy divorce law to protect them.

Awhile ago I said that M. Bourget's method of
truth-seeking — hunting for it in out-of-the-way
places — was new; but that was an error. I remember that when Leverrier discovered the Milky
Way, he and the other astronomers began to theorize
about it in substantially the same fashion which M.
Bourget employs in his reasonings about American
social facts and their origin. Leverrier advanced
the hypothesis that the Milky Way was caused by
gaseous protoplasmic emanations from the field of
Waterloo, which, ascending to an altitude determin-
able by their own specific gravity, became luminous
through the development and exposure — by the
natural processes of animal decay — of the phos-
phorus contained in them.

A LITTLE NOTE TO M. PAUL BOURGET

[The preceding squib was assailed in the *North American Review* in an article entitled "Mark Twain and Paul Bourget," by Max O'Rell. The following little note is a Rejoinder to that article. It is possible that the position assumed here — that M. Bourget dictated the O'Rell article himself — is untenable.]

YOU have every right, my dear M. Bourget, to retort upon me by dictation, if you prefer that method to writing at me with your pen; but if I may say it without hurt — and certainly I mean no offence — I believe you would have acquitted yourself better with the pen. With the pen you are at home; it is your natural weapon; you use it with grace, eloquence, charm, persuasiveness, when men are to be convinced, and with formidable effect when they have earned a castigation. But I am sure I see signs in the above article that you are either unaccustomed to dictating or are out of practice. If you will re-read it you will notice, yourself, that it lacks definiteness; that it lacks purpose; that it lacks coherence; that it lacks a subject to talk about; that it is loose and wabbly; that it wanders around; that it loses itself early and does not find itself any more. There are some other defects, as you will

(165)

Reply yourself.   I knew you did it to save yourself manual labor.

And you had the right, as I have already said; and I am content — perfectly content. Yet it would have been little trouble to you, and a great kindness to me, if you had written your Reply all out with your own capable hand.

Because then it would have replied — and that is really what a Reply is for. Broadly speaking, its function is to refute — as you will easily concede. That leaves something for the other person to take hold of: he has a chance to reply to the Reply, he has a chance to refute the refutation. This would have happened if you had written it out instead of dictating.   Dictating is nearly sure to unconcentrate the dictator's mind, when he is out of practice, confuse him, and betray him into using one set of literary rules when he ought to use a quite different set. Often it betrays him into employing the RULES FOR CONVERSATION BETWEEN A SHOUTER AND A DEAF PERSON — as in the present case — when he ought to employ the RULES FOR CONDUCTING DISCUSSION WITH A FAULT-FINDER. The great foundation-rule and basic principle of discussion with a fault-finder is relevancy and concentration upon the subject; whereas the great foundation-rule and basic principle governing conversation between a shouter and a deaf person is irrelevancy and persistent desertion of the topic in hand. If I may be allowed to illustrate by quoting example IV., section 7,

from chapter ix. of " Revised Rules for Conducting
Conversation between a Shouter and a Deaf Person," it will assist us in getting a clear idea of the
difference between the two sets of rules :

Shouter.   Did you say his name is WETHERBY?

Deaf Person.   Change?   Yes, I think it will.
Though if it should clear off I —

Shouter.   It's his NAME I want — his NAME.

Deaf Person.   Maybe so, maybe so; but it will
only be a shower, I think.

Shouter.   No, no, *no!* — you have quite mis-
underSTOOD me.   If —

Deaf Person.   Ah! GOOD morning; I am sorry
you must go.   But call again, and let me continue
to be of assistance to you in every way I can.

You see it is a perfect kodak of the article you
have dictated.   It is really curious and interesting
when you come to compare it with yours; in detail,
with my former article to which it is a Reply in
your hand.   I talk twelve pages about your American instruction projects, and your doubtful scientific
system, and your painstaking classification of non-
existent things, and your diligence and zeal and
sincerity, and your disloyal attitude towards anec-
dotes, and your undue reverence for unsafe statistics
and for facts that lack a pedigree; and you turn
around and come back at me with eight pages of
weather.

I do not see how a person can act so.   It is good
of you to repeat, with change of language, in the

It relates to manners, customs, and morals — three
things concerning which we can never have ex-
haustive and determinate statistics, and so the
verdicts delivered upon them must always lack con-
clusiveness and be subject to revision; but you have
stated the truth, possibly, as nearly as any one
could do it, in the circumstances.   But why did you
choose a detail of my question which could be
answered only with vague hearsay evidence, and
go right by one which could have been answered
with deadly facts? — facts in everybody's reach,
facts which none can dispute.   I asked what France
could teach us about government.   I laid myself
pretty wide open, there; and I thought I was hand-
somely generous, too, when I did it.   France can
teach us how to levy village and city taxes which
distribute the burden with a nearer approach to perfect fairness than is the case in any other land; and
she can teach us the wisest and surest system of collecting them that exists.   She can teach us how to
elect a President in a sane way; and also how to do
it without throwing the country into earthquakes
and convulsions that cripple and embarrass business,
stir up party hatred in the hearts of men, and make

his club would immediately see his name canceled from membership.   A
man who had settled his fortune on his wife to avoid meeting his creditors would be refused admission into any decent society.   Many a
Frenchman has blown his brains out rather than declare himself a bankrupt.   Now would Mark Twain remark to this: "An American is not
such a fool: when a creditor stands in his way he closes his doors, and
reopens them the following day.   When he has been a bankrupt three
times he can retire from business?"

peaceful people wish the term extended to thirty years. France can teach us — but enough of that part of the question. And what else can France teach us? She can teach us all the fine arts — and does. She throws open her hospitable art academies, and says to us, " Come " — and we come, troops and troops of our young and gifted; and she sets over us the ablest masters in the world and bearing the greatest names; and she teaches us all that we are capable of learning, and persuades us and encourages us with prizes and honors, much as if we were somehow children of her own; and when this noble education is finished and we are ready to carry it home and spread its gracious ministries abroad over our nation, and we come with homage and gratitude and ask France for the bill — *there is nothing to pay*. And in return for this imperial generosity, what does America do? She charges a duty on French works of art!

I wish I had your end of this dispute; I should have something worth talking about. If you would only furnish me something to argue, something to refute — but you persistently won't. You leave good chances unutilized and spend your strength in proving and establishing unimportant things. For instance, you have proven and established these eight facts here following — a good score as to number, but not worth while:

Mark Twain is —

1. " Insulting."

12E

2. (Sarcastically speaking) " This refined humorist."

3. Prefers the manure-pile to the violets.

4. Has uttered " an ill-natured sneer."

5. Is " nasty."

6. Needs a " lesson in politeness and good manners."

7. Has published a " nasty article."

8. Has made remarks " unworthy of a gentleman."* These are all true, but really they are not
valuable; no one cares much for such finds. In
our American magazines we recognize this and sup-
press them. We avoid naming them. American
writers never allow themselves to name them. It
would look as if they were in a temper, and we hold
that exhibitions of temper in public are not good
form — except in the very young and inexperienced.
And even if we had the disposition to name them,

---

* " It is more funny than his " (Mark Twain's) " anecdote, and
would have been less insulting."

A quoted remark of mine " is a gross insult to a nation friendly to
America."

" He has read *La Terre*, this refined humorist."

" When Mark Twain visits a garden . . . he goes in the far-away
corner where the soil is prepared."

" Mark Twain's ill-natured sneer cannot so much as stain them "
(the Frenchwomen).

" When he " (Mark Twain) " takes his revenge he is unkind, unfair, bitter, nasty."

" But not even your nasty article on my country, Mark," etc.

" Mark might certainly have derived from it " (M. Bourget's book)
" a lesson in politeness and good manners."

A quoted remark of mine is " unworthy of a gentleman."

in order to fill up a gap when we were short of ideas
and arguments, our magazines would not allow us to
do it, because they think that such words sully their
pages.   This present magazine is particularly strenuous about it.   Its note to me announcing the
forwarding of your proof-sheets to France closed
thus — for your protection:

   " *It is needless to ask you to avoid anything that
he might consider as personal.*"

   It was well enough, as a measure of precaution,
but really it was not needed.   You can trust me im-
plicitly, M. Bourget; I shall never call you any
names in print which I should be ashamed to call
you with your unoffending and dearest ones present.

   Indeed, we are reserved, and particular in America
to a degree which you would consider exaggerated.
For instance, we should not write notes like that one
of yours to a lady for a small fault — or a large
one.*   We should not think it kind.   No matter

---

   * When M. Paul Bourget indulges in a little chaffing at the expense
of the Americans, " who can always get away with a few years' trying
to find out who their grandfathers were," he merely makes an allusion
to an American foible; but, forsooth, what a kind man, what a humorist Mark Twain is when he retorts by calling France a nation of
bastards!   How the Americans of culture and refinement will admire
him for thus speaking in their name!

   Snobbery. . . . I could give Mark Twain an example of the American specimen.   It is a piquant story.   I never published it because I
feared my readers might think that I was giving them a typical illustra-
tion of American character instead of a rare exception.

   I was once booked by my manager to give a *causerie* in the drawing-
room of a New York millionaire.   I accepted with reluctance.   I do

how much we might have associated with kings and nobilities, we should not think it right to crush her with it and make her ashamed of her lowlier walk in life; for we have a saying, "Who humiliates my mother includes his own."

Do I seriously imagine you to be the author of that strange letter, M. Bourget? Indeed I do not. I believe it to have been surreptitiously inserted by your amanuensis when your back was turned. I think he did it with a good motive, expecting it to

---

not like private engagements. At five o'clock on the day the *causerie* was to be given, the lady sent to my manager to say that she would expect me to arrive at nine o'clock and to speak for about an hour. Then she wrote a postscript. Many women are unfortunate there. Their minds are full of after-thoughts, and the most important part of their letters is generally to be found after their signature. This lady's P. S. ran thus: "I suppose he will not expect to be entertained after the lecture."

I fairly shouted, as Mark Twain would say, and then, indulging myself in a bit of snobbishness, I was back at her as quick as a flash—

"Dear Madam: As a literary man of some reputation, I have many times had the pleasure of being entertained by the members of the old aristocracy of France. I have also many times had the pleasure of being entertained by the members of the old aristocracy of England. If it may interest you, I can even tell you that I have several times had the honor of being entertained by royalty; but my ambition has never been so wild as to expect that one day I might be entertained by the aristocracy of New York. No, I do not expect to be entertained by you, nor do I want you to expect me to entertain you and your friends to-night, for I decline to keep the engagement."

Now, I could fill a book on America with reminiscences of this sort, adding a few chapters on bosses and boodlers, on New York *chronique scandaleuse*, on the tenement houses of the large cities, on the gambling-hells of Denver, and the dens of San Francisco, and what not! But not even your nasty article on my country, Mark, will make me do it.

add force and piquancy to your article, but it does not reflect your nature, and I know it will grieve you when you see it.   I also think he interlarded many other things which you will disapprove of when you see them.   I am certain that all the harsh names discharged at me come from him, not you. No doubt you could have proved me entitled to them with as little trouble as it has cost him to do it, but it would have been your disposition to hunt game of a higher quality.

Why, I even doubt if it is you who furnish me all that excellent information about Balzac and those others.*   All this in simple justice to you — and to me; for, to gravely accept those interlardings as yours would be to wrong your head and heart, and at the same time convict myself of being equipped

---

* "Now the style of M. Bourget and many other French writers is apparently a closed letter to Mark Twain; but let us leave that alone. Has he read Erckmann-Chatrian, Victor Hugo, Lamartine, Edmond About, Cherbuliez, Renan?   Has he read Gustave Droz's *Monsieur, Madame, et Bébé,* and those books which leave for a long time a perfume about you?   Has he read the novels of Alexandre Dumas, Eugène Sue, George Sand, and Balzac?   Has he read Victor Hugo's *Les Misérables* and *Notre Dame de Paris?*   Has he read or heard the plays of Sandeau, Augier, Dumas, and Sardou, the works of those Titans of modern literature, whose names will be household words all over the world for hundreds of years to come?   He has read *La Terre*—this kind-hearted, refined humorist!   When Mark Twain visits a garden does he smell the violets, the roses, the jasmine, or the honeysuckle? No, he goes in the far-away corner where the soil is prepared.   Hear what he says: "I wish M. Paul Bourget had read more of our novels before he came.   It is the only way to thoroughly understand a people. When I found I was coming to Paris I read *La Terre*."

12*₊*₊

with a vacancy where my penetration ought to be lodged.

And now finally I must uncover the secret pain, the wee sore from which the Reply grew —*the anecdote which closed my recent article*—and consider how it is that this pimple has spread to these cancerous dimensions. If any but you had dictated the Reply, M. Bourget, I would know that that anecdote was twisted around and its intention magnified some hundreds of times, in order that it might be used as a pretext to creep in the back way. But I accuse you of nothing — nothing but error. When you say that I '' retort by calling France a nation of bastards,'' it is an error. And not a small one, but a large one. I made no such remark, nor anything resembling it. Moreover, the magazine would not have allowed me to use so gross a word as that.

You told an anecdote. A funny one—I admit that. It hit a foible of our American aristocracy, and it stung me — I admit that; it stung me sharply. It was like this: You found some ancient portraits of French kings in the gallery of one of our aristocracy, and you said:

'' He has the Grand Monarch, but *where is the portrait of his grandfather?*'' That is, the American aristocrat's grandfather.

Now that hits only a few of us, I grant — just the upper crust only — but it hits exceedingly hard.

I wondered if there was any way of getting back at you. In one of your chapters I found this chance:

"In our high Parisian existence, for instance, we find applied to arts and luxury, and to debauchery, all the powers and all the weaknesses of the French soul."

You see? Your "higher Parisian" class — not everybody, not the nation, but only the *top crust* of the nation — *applies to debauchery all the powers of its soul*.

I argued to myself that that energy must produce results. So I built an anecdote out of your remark. In it I make Napoleon Bonaparte say to me — but see for yourself the anecdote (ingeniously clipped and curtailed) in paragraph eleven of your Reply.*

---

* So, I repeat, Mark Twain does not like M. Paul Bourget's book. So long as he makes light fun of the great French writer he is at home, he is pleasant, he is the American humorist we know. When he takes his revenge (and where is the reason for taking a revenge?) he is unkind, unfair, bitter, nasty.

For example:

See his answer to a Frenchman who jokingly remarks to him:

"I suppose life can never get entirely dull to an American, because whenever he can't strike up any other way to put in his time, he can always get away with a few years trying to find out who his grandfather was."

Hear the answer:

"I reckon a Frenchman's got *his* little standby for a dull time, too; because when all other interests fail, he can turn in and see if he can't find out who his father was."

The first remark is a good-humored bit of chaffing on American snobbery. I may be utterly destitute of humor, but I call the second remark a gratuitous charge of immorality hurled at the French women — a remark unworthy of a man who has the ear of the public, unworthy of a gentleman, a gross insult to a nation friendly to America, a nation that helped Mark Twain's ancestors in their struggle for liberty, a nation

L*₊*₊

to say, I know *now* that it was Limburger cheese, but at that time I never had heard of the article in my life, and of course was wholly ignorant of its character. Well, we sped through the wild night, the bitter storm raged on, a cheerless misery stole over me, my heart went down, down, down! The old expressman made a brisk remark or two about the tempest and the arctic weather, slammed his sliding doors to, and bolted them, closed his window down tight, and then went bustling around, here and there and yonder, setting things to rights, and all the time contentedly humming " Sweet By and By,'' in a low tone, and flatting a good deal. Presently I began to detect a most evil and searching odor stealing about on the frozen air. This depressed my spirits still more, because of course I attributed it to my poor departed friend. There was something infinitely saddening about his calling himself to my remembrance in this dumb pathetic way, so it was hard to keep the tears back. Moreover, it distressed me on account of the old expressman, who, I was afraid, might notice it. However, he went humming tranquilly on, and gave no sign; and for this I was grateful. Grateful, yes, but still uneasy; and soon I began to feel more and more uneasy every minute, for every minute that went by that odor thickened up the more, and got to be more and more gamey and hard to stand. Presently, having got things arranged to his satisfaction, the expressman got some wood and made up a tremendous fire in his stove.

This distressed me more than I can tell, for I could not but feel that it was a mistake. I was sure that the effect would be deleterious upon my poor departed friend. Thompson — the expressman's name was Thompson, as I found out in the course of the night — now went poking around his car, stopping up whatever stray cracks he could find, remarking that it didn't make any difference what kind of a night it was outside, he calculated to make *us* comfortable, anyway. I said nothing, but I believed he was not choosing the right way. Meantime he was humming to himself just as before; and meantime, too, the stove was getting hotter and hotter, and the place closer and closer. I felt myself growing pale and qualmish, but grieved in silence and said nothing. Soon I noticed that the " Sweet By and By " was gradually fading out; next it ceased altogether, and there was an ominous stillness. After a few moments Thompson said,—

" Pfew! I reckon it ain't no cinnamon 't I've loaded up thish-yer stove with!"

He gasped once or twice, then moved toward the cof—gun-box, stood over that Limburger cheese part of a moment, then came back and sat down near me, looking a good deal impressed. After a contemplative pause, he said, indicating the box with a gesture,—

" Friend of yourn ?"

" Yes," I said with a sigh.

" He's pretty ripe, *ain't* he!"

" I've carried a many a one of 'em,— some of 'em considerable overdue, too,— but, lordy, he just lays over 'em all! — and does it *easy*. Cap., they was heliotrope to *him!*"

This recognition of my poor friend gratified me, in spite of the sad circumstances, because it had so much the sound of a compliment.

Pretty soon it was plain that something had got to be done. I suggested cigars. Thompson thought it was a good idea. He said,—

" Likely it'll modify him some."

We puffed gingerly along for a while, and tried hard to imagine that things were improved. But it wasn't any use. Before very long, and without any consultation, both cigars were quietly dropped from our nerveless fingers at the same moment. Thompson said, with a sigh,—

" No, Cap., it don't modify him worth a cent. Fact is, it makes him worse, becuz it appears to stir up his ambition. What do you reckon we better do, now?"

I was not able to suggest anything; indeed, I had to be swallowing and swallowing, all the time, and did not like to trust myself to speak. Thompson fell to maundering, in a desultory and low-spirited way, about the miserable experiences of this night; and he got to referring to my poor friend by various titles,— sometimes military ones, sometimes civil ones; and I noticed that as fast as my poor friend's effectiveness grew, Thompson promoted him accordingly,— gave him a bigger title. Finally he said,—

"I've got an idea. Suppos'n we buckle down to it and give the Colonel a bit of a shove towards t'other end of the car? — about ten foot, say. He wouldn't have so much influence, then, don't you reckon?"

I said it was a good scheme. So we took in a good fresh breath at the broken pane, calculating to hold it till we got through; then we went there and bent over that deadly cheese and took a grip on the box. Thompson nodded "All ready," and then we threw ourselves forward with all our might; but Thompson slipped, and slumped down with his nose on the cheese, and his breath got loose. He gagged and gasped, and floundered up and made a break for the door, pawing the air and saying hoarsely, "Don't hender me! — gimme the road! I'm a-dying; gimme the road!" Out on the cold platform I sat down and held his head a while, and he revived. Presently he said,—

"Do you reckon we started the Gen'rul any?"

I said no; we hadn't budged him.

"Well, then, *that* idea's up the flume. We got to think up something else. He's suited wher' he is, I reckon; and if that's the way he feels about it, and has made up his mind that he don't wish to be disturbed, you bet he's a-going to have his own way in the business. Yes, better leave him right wher' he is, long as he wants it so; becuz he holds all the

13E

trumps, don't you know, and so it stands to reason
that the man that lays out to alter his plans for him
is going to get left.''

But we couldn't stay out there in that mad storm;
we should have frozen to death. So we went in
again and shut the door, and began to suffer once
more and take turns at the break in the window. By
and by, as we were starting away from a station where
we had stopped a moment Thompson pranced in
cheerily, and exclaimed,—

"We're all right, now! I reckon we've got the
Commodore this time. I judge I've got the stuff
here that'll take the tuck out of him.''

It was carbolic acid. He had a carboy of it. He
sprinkled it all around everywhere; in fact he
drenched everything with it, rifle-box, cheese and all.
Then we sat down, feeling pretty hopeful. But it
wasn't for long. You see the two perfumes began
to mix, and then — well, pretty soon we made a
break for the door; and out there Thompson swabbed
his face with his bandanna and said in a kind of dis-
heartened way,—

"It ain't no use. We can't buck agin *him*. He
just utilizes everything we put up to modify him with,
and gives it his own flavor and plays it back on us.
Why, Cap., don't you know, it's as much as a
hundred times worse in there now than it was when
he first got a-going. I never *did* see one of 'em
warm up to his work so, and take such a dumnation
interest in it. No, sir, I never did, as long as I've

THESE GAVE IT A BETTER HOLD

ben on the road; and I've carried a many a one of 'em, as I was telling you."

We went in again after we were frozen pretty stiff; but my, we couldn't *stay* in, now. So we just waltzed back and forth, freezing, and thawing, and stifling, by turns. In about an hour we stopped at another station; and as we left it Thompson came in with a bag, and said,—

"Cap., I'm a-going to chance him once more,— just this once; and if we don't fetch him this time, the thing for us to do, is to just throw up the sponge and withdraw from the canvass. That's the way *I* put it up."

He had brought a lot of chicken feathers, and dried apples, and leaf tobacco, and rags, and old shoes, and sulphur, and asafœtida, and one thing or another; and he piled them on a breadth of sheet iron in the middle of the floor, and set fire to them.

When they got well started, I couldn't see, myself, how even the corpse could stand it. All that went before was just simply poetry to that smell,—but mind you, the original smell stood up out of it just as sublime as ever,—fact is, these other smells just seemed to give it a better hold; and my, how rich it was! I didn't make these reflections there — there wasn't time — made them on the platform. And breaking for the platform, Thompson got suffocated and fell; and before I got him dragged out, which I did by the collar, I was mighty near gone myself. When we revived, Thompson said dejectedly,—

" We got to stay out here, Cap.   We got to do it. They ain't no other way.   The Governor wants to travel alone, and he's fixed so he can outvote us."

And presently he added,—

" And don't you know, we're *pisoned*.   It's *our* last trip, you can make up your mind to it.   Typhoid fever is what's going to come of this.   I feel it a-coming right now.   Yes, sir, we're elected, just as sure as you're born."

We were taken from the platform an hour later, frozen and insensible, at the next station, and I went straight off into a virulent fever, and never knew anything again for three weeks.   I found out, then, that I had spent that awful night with a harmless box of rifles and a lot of innocent cheese ; but the news was too late to save *me;* imagination had done its work, and my health was permanently shattered ; neither Bermuda nor any other land can ever bring it back to me.   This is my last trip ; I am on my way home to die.

THE CAPTAIN'S STORY

THERE was a good deal of pleasant gossip about old Captain " Hurricane " Jones, of the Pacific Ocean,— peace to his ashes! Two or three of us present had known him; I, particularly well, for I had made four sea-voyages with him. He was a very remarkable man. He was born on a ship; he picked up what little education he had among his shipmates; he began life in the forecastle, and climbed grade by grade to the captaincy. More than fifty years of his sixty-five were spent at sea. He had sailed all oceans, seen all lands, and borrowed a tint from all climates. When a man has been fifty years at sea, he necessarily knows nothing of men, nothing of the world but its surface, nothing of the world's thought, nothing of the world's learning but its A B C, and that blurred and distorted by the unfocused lenses of an untrained mind. Such a man is only a gray and bearded child. That is what old Hurricane Jones was,— simply an innocent, lovable old infant. When his spirit was in repose he was as sweet and gentle as a girl; when his wrath was up he was a hurricane

13*.*.   (193)

that made his nickname seem tamely descriptive.
He was formidable in a fight, for he was of powerful
build and dauntless courage.   He was frescoed from
head to heel with pictures and mottoes tattooed in
red and blue India ink.   I was with him one voyage
when he got his last vacant space tattooed;   this
vacant space was around his left ankle.   During
three days he stumped about the ship with his ankle
bare and swollen, and this legend gleaming red and
angry out from a clouding of India ink: " Virtue is
its own R'd." (There was a lack of room.)   He
was deeply and sincerely pious, and swore like a
fish-woman.   He considered swearing blameless,
because sailors would not understand an order un-
illumined by it. He was a profound Biblical scholar,
— that is, he thought he was.   He believed everything in the Bible, but he had his own methods of
arriving at his beliefs.   He was of the " advanced "
school of thinkers, and applied natural laws to the
interpretation of all miracles, somewhat on the plan
of the people who make the six days of creation six
geological epochs, and so forth.   Without being
aware of it, he was a rather severe satire on modern
scientific religionists.   Such a man as I have been
describing is rabidly fond of disquisition and argument; one knows that without being told it.

One trip the captain had a clergyman on board,
but did not know he was a clergyman, since the
passenger list did not betray the fact.   He took
a great liking to this Rev. Mr. Peters, and talked

with him a great deal: told him yarns, gave him
toothsome scraps of personal history, and wove a
glittering streak of profanity through his garru-
lous fabric that was refreshing to a spirit weary
of the dull neutralities of undecorated speech. One
day the captain said, " Peters, do you ever read
the Bible?"

" Well — yes."

" I judge it ain't often, by the way you say it.
Now, you tackle it in dead earnest once, and you'll
find it'll pay. Don't you get discouraged, but hang
right on. First, you won't understand it; but by
and by things will begin to clear up, and then you
wouldn't lay it down to eat."

" Yes, I have heard that said."

" And it's so, too. There ain't a book that begins
with it. It lays over 'em all, Peters. There's some
pretty tough things in it,— there ain't any getting
around that,— but you stick to them and think them
out, and when once you get on the inside everything's plain as day."

" The miracles, too, captain?"

" Yes, sir! the miracles, too. Every one of them.
Now, there's that business with the prophets of
Baal; like enough that stumped you?"

" Well, I don't know but —"

" Own up, now; it stumped you. Well, I don't
wonder. You hadn't had any experience in raveling
such things out, and naturally it was too many for
you. Would you like to have me explain that thing

M*.*.

to you, and show you how to get at the meat of these matters?''

" Indeed, I would, captain, if you don't mind.''

Then the captain proceeded as follows: " I'll do it with pleasure.   First, you see, I read and read, and thought and thought, till I got to understand what sort of people they were in the old Bible times, and then after that it was clear and easy.   Now, this was the way I put it up, concerning Isaac* and the prophets of Baal.   There was some mighty sharp men amongst the public characters of that old ancient day, and Isaac was one of them.   Isaac had his failings,— plenty of them, too; it ain't for me to apologize for Isaac; he played on the prophets of Baal, and like enough he was justifiable, considering the odds that was against him.   No, all I say is, 't wa'n't any miracle, and that I'll show you so's't you can see it yourself.

" Well, times had been getting rougher and rougher for prophets,— that is, prophets of Isaac's denomination.   There were four hundred and fifty prophets of Baal in the community, and only one Presbyterian; that is, if Isaac *was* a Presbyterian, which I reckon he was, but it don't say.   Naturally, the prophets of Baal took all the trade.   Isaac was pretty low-spirited, I reckon, but he was a good deal of a man, and no doubt he went a-prophesying around, letting on to be doing a land-office busi-

---

* This is the captain's own mistake.

ness, but 'twa'n't any use; he couldn't run any opposition to amount to anything. By and by things got desperate with him; he sets his head to work and thinks it all out, and then what does he do? Why, he begins to throw out hints that the other parties are this and that and t'other,— nothing very definite, may be, but just kind of undermining their reputation in a quiet way. This made talk, of course, and finally got to the king. The king asked Isaac what he meant by his talk. Says Isaac, 'Oh, nothing particular; only, can they pray down fire from heaven on an altar? It ain't much, maybe, your majesty, only can they *do* it? That's the idea.' So the king was a good deal disturbed, and he went to the prophets of Baal, and they said, pretty airy, that if he had an altar ready, *they* were ready; and they intimated he better get it insured, too.

"So next morning all the children of Israel and their parents and the other people gathered themselves together. Well, here was that great crowd of prophets of Baal packed together on one side, and Isaac walking up and down all alone on the other, putting up his job. When time was called, Isaac let on to be comfortable and indifferent; told the other team to take the first innings. So they went at it, the whole four hundred and fifty, praying around the altar, very hopeful, and doing their level best. They prayed an hour,— two hours,— three hours,— and so on, plumb till noon. It wa'n't any use; they

STIRRING TIMES IN AUSTRIA

I. THE GOVERNMENT IN THE FRYING-PAN

HERE in Vienna in these closing days of 1897
one's blood gets no chance to stagnate. The
atmosphere is brimful of political electricity. All
conversation is political; every man is a battery,
with brushes overworn, and gives out blue sparks
when you set him going on the common topic.
Everybody has an opinion, and lets you have it
frank and hot, and out of this multitude of counsel you get merely confusion and despair. For
no one really understands this political situation,
or can tell you what is going to be the outcome
of it.

Things have happened here recently which
would set any country but Austria on fire from
end to end, and upset the government to a
certainty; but no one feels confident that such
results will follow here. Here, apparently, one
must wait and see what will happen, then
he will know, and not before; guessing is
idle; guessing cannot help the matter. This is

(200)

what the wise tell you; they all say it; they say it every day, and it is the sole detail upon which they all agree.

There is some approach to agreement upon another point: that there will be no revolution. Men say: "Look at our history — revolutions have not been in our line; and look at our political map — its construction is unfavorable to an organized uprising, and without unity what could a revolt accomplish? It is *dis*union which has held our empire together for centuries, and what it has done in the past it may continue to do now and in the future."

The most intelligible sketch I have encountered of this unintelligible arrangement of things was contributed to the *Travelers Record* by Mr. Forrest Morgan, of Hartford, three years ago. He says:

The Austro-Hungarian Monarchy is the patchwork quilt, the Midway Plaisance, the national chain-gang of Europe; a state that is not a nation but a collection of nations, some with national memories and aspirations and others without, some occupying distinct provinces almost purely their own, and others mixed with alien races, but each with a different language, and each mostly holding the others foreigners as much as if the link of a common government did not exist. Only one of its races even now comprises so much as *one-fourth* of the whole, and not another so much as *one-sixth;* and each has remained for ages as unchanged in isolation, however mingled together in locality, as globules of oil in water. There is nothing else in the modern world that is nearly like it, though there have been plenty in past ages; it seems unreal and impossible even though we know it is true; it violates all our feeling as to what a country should be in order to have a right to exist; and it seems as though it was too ramshackle to go on holding together any length of time. Yet it has survived, much in its present shape, two is suppressed in one paper fails to be damned in another one, and gets published in full feather and unmodified. Then the paper in which it was suppressed blandly copies the forbidden matter into its evening edition — provokingly giving credit and detailing all the circumstances in courteous and inoffensive language — and of course the censor cannot say a word.

Sometimes the censor sucks all the blood out of a newspaper and leaves it colorless and inane; sometimes he leaves it undisturbed, and lets it talk out its opinions with a frankness and vigor hardly to be surpassed, I think, in the journals of any country. Apparently the censor sometimes revises his verdicts upon second thought, for several times lately he has suppressed journals after their issue and partial distribution. The distributed copies are then sent for by the censor and destroyed. I have two of these, but at the time they were sent for I could not remember what I had done with them.

If the censor did his work before the morning edition was printed, he would be less of an inconvenience than he is; but of course the papers cannot wait many minutes after five o'clock to get his verdict; they might as well go out of business as do that; so they print, and take the chances. Then, if they get caught by a suppression, they must strike out the condemned matter and print the edition over again. That delays the issue several hours, and is expensive besides. The government gets the sup-

pressed edition for nothing. If it bought it, that
would be joyful, and would give great satisfaction.
Also, the edition would be larger. Some of the
papers do not replace the condemned paragraphs
with other matter; they merely snatch them out and
leave blanks behind — mourning blanks, marked
" *Confiscated.*"

The government discourages the dissemination of
newspaper information in other ways. For instance,
it does not allow newspapers to be sold on the streets;
therefore the newsboy is unknown in Vienna. And
there is a stamp duty of nearly a cent upon each
copy of a newspaper's issue. Every American paper
that reaches me has a stamp upon it, which has been
pasted there in the post-office or downstairs in the
hotel office; but no matter who put it there, I have
to pay for it, and that is the main thing. Sometimes
friends send me so many papers that it takes all I
can earn that week to keep this government going.

I must take passing notice of another point in the
government's measures for maintaining tranquillity.
Everybody says it does not like to see any individual
attain to commanding influence in the country, since
such a man can become a disturber and an inconvenience. " We have as much talent as the other
nations," says the citizen, resignedly, and without
bitterness, " but for the sake of the general good of
the country we are discouraged from making it over-
conspicuous; and not only discouraged, but tactfully
and skillfully prevented from doing it, if we show

14E

too much persistence.   Consequently we have no
renowned men; in centuries we have seldom pro-
duced one — that is, seldom allowed one to produce
himself.   We can say to-day what no other nation
of first importance in the family of Christian civil-
izations can say: that there exists no Austrian who
has made an enduring name for himself which is familiar all around the globe.''

Another helper toward tranquillity is the army. It
is as pervasive as the atmosphere.   It is everywhere.
All the mentioned creators, promoters, and pre-
servers of the public tranquillity do their several
shares in the quieting work.   They make a restful
and comfortable serenity and reposefulness.   This is
disturbed sometimes for a little while: a mob as-
sembles to protest against something; it gets noisy
— noisier — still noisier — finally *too* noisy; then
the persuasive soldiery come charging down upon it,
and in a few minutes all is quiet again, and there is
no mob.

There is a Constitution and there is a Parliament.
The House draws its membership of 425 deputies
from the nineteen or twenty states heretofore mentioned.   These men represent peoples who speak
eleven languages.   That means eleven distinct varie-
ties of jealousies, hostilities, and warring interests.
This could be expected to furnish forth a parliament of a pretty inharmonious sort, and make legis-
lation difficult at times — and it does that.   The
parliament is split up into many parties — the Cler-

icals, the Progressists, the German Nationalists, the Young Czechs, the Social Democrats, the Christian Socialists, and some others — and it is difficult to get up working combinations among them. They prefer to fight apart sometimes.

The recent troubles have grown out of Count Badeni's necessities. He could not carry on his government without a majority vote in the House at his back, and in order to secure it he had to make a trade of some sort. He made it with the Czechs — the Bohemians. The terms were not easy for him: he must pass a bill making the Czech tongue the official language in Bohemia in place of the German. This created a storm. All the Germans in Austria were incensed. In numbers they form but a fourth part of the empire's population, but they urge that the country's public business should be conducted in one common tongue, and that tongue a world language — which German is.

However, Badeni secured his majority. The German element in parliament was apparently become helpless. The Czech deputies were exultant.

Then the music began. Badeni's voyage, instead of being smooth, was disappointingly rough from the start. The government must get the *Ausgleich* through. It must not fail. Badeni's majority was ready to carry it through; but the minority was determined to obstruct it and delay it until the obnoxious Czech-language measure should be shelved.

The *Ausgleich* is an Adjustment, Arrangement, Settlement, which holds Austria and Hungary together. It dates from 1867, and has to be renewed every ten years. It establishes the share which Hungary must pay toward the expenses of the imperial government. Hungary is a kingdom (the Emperor of Austria is its King), and has its own parliament and governmental machinery. But it has no foreign office, and it has no army — at least its army is a part of the imperial army, is paid out of the imperial treasury, and is under the control of the imperial war office.

The ten-year rearrangement was due a year ago, but failed to connect. At least completely. A year's compromise was arranged. A new arrangement must be effected before the last day of this year. Otherwise the two countries become separate entities. The Emperor would still be King of Hungary — that is, King of an independent foreign country. There would be Hungarian custom-houses on the Austrian frontier, and there would be a Hungarian army and a Hungarian foreign office. Both countries would be weakened by this, both would suffer damage.

The Opposition in the House, although in the minority, had a good weapon to fight with in the pending *Ausgleich*. If it could delay the *Ausgleich* a few weeks, the government would doubtless have to withdraw the hated language bill or lose Hungary.

The Opposition began its fight. Its arms were the Rules of the House. It was soon manifest that by applying these Rules ingeniously it could make the majority helpless, and keep it so as long as it pleased. It could shut off business every now and then with a motion to adjourn. It could require the ayes and noes on the motion, and use up thirty minutes on that detail. It could call for the reading and verification of the minutes of the preceding meeting, and use up half a day in that way. It could require that several of its members be entered upon the list of permitted speakers previously to the opening of a sitting; and as there is no time limit, further delays could thus be accomplished.

These were all lawful weapons, and the men of the Opposition (technically called the Left) were within their rights in using them. They used them to such dire purpose that all parliamentary business was paralyzed. The Right (the government side) could accomplish nothing. Then it had a saving idea. This idea was a curious one. It was to have the President and the Vice-Presidents of the parliament trample the Rules under foot upon occasion !

This, for a profoundly embittered minority constructed out of fire and gun-cotton ! It was time for idle strangers to go and ask leave to look down out of a gallery and see what would be the result of it.

14*.*.*

II. A MEMORABLE SITTING

And now took place that memorable sitting of the House which broke two records. It lasted the best part of two days and a night, surpassing by half an hour the longest sitting known to the world's previous parliamentary history, and breaking the long-speech record with Dr. Lecher's twelve-hour effort, the longest flow of unbroken talk that ever came out of one mouth since the world began.

At 8:45, on the evening of the 28th of October, when the House had been sitting a few minutes short of ten hours, Dr. Lecher was granted the floor. It was a good place for theatrical effects. I think that no other Senate House is so shapely as this one, or so richly and showily decorated. Its plan is that of an opera-house. Up toward the straight side of it — the stage side — rise a couple of terraces of desks for the ministry, and the official clerks or secretaries — terraces thirty feet long, and each supporting about half a dozen desks with spaces between them. Above these is the President's terrace, against the wall. Along it are distributed the proper accommodations for the presiding officer and his assistants. The wall is of richly colored marble highly polished, its paneled sweep relieved by fluted columns and pilasters of distinguished grace and dignity, which glow softly and frostily in the electric light. Around the spacious half-circle of the floor bends the great two-storied curve of the boxes, its frontage elaborately ornamented and sumptuously gilded. On the floor of the House the 425 desks radiate fanwise from the President's tribune.

The galleries are crowded on this particular evening, for word has gone about that the *Ausgleich* is before the House; that the President, Ritter von Abraham-owicz, has been throttling the Rules; that the Opposition are in an inflammable state in consequence, and that the night session is likely to be of an exciting sort.

The gallery guests are fashionably dressed, and the finery of the women makes a bright and pretty show under the strong electric light. But down on the floor there is no costumery.

The deputies are dressed in day clothes; some of the clothes neat and trim, others not; there may be three members in evening dress, but not more. There are several Catholic priests in their long black gowns, and with crucifixes hanging from their necks. No member wears his hat. One may see by these details that the aspects are not those of an evening sitting of an English House of Commons, but rather those of a sitting of our House of Representatives.

In his high place sits the President, Abrahamowicz, object of the Opposition's limitless hatred. He is sunk back in the depths of his arm-chair, and has his chin down. He brings the ends of his spread fingers together in front of his breast, and reflectively taps them together, with the air of one who would like to begin business, but must wait, and be as patient as he can. It makes you think of Richelieu. Now

N*₄*₄

The tempest burst out again; yells of approval from the Left, catcalls, an ironical laughter from the Right. At this point a new and most effective noisemaker was pressed into service. Each desk has an extension, consisting of a removable board eighteen inches long, six wide, and a half-inch thick. A member pulled one of these out and began to belabor the top of his desk with it. Instantly other members followed suit, and perhaps you can imagine the result. Of all conceivable rackets it is the most ear-splitting, intolerable, and altogether fiendish.

The persecuted President leaned back in his chair, closed his eyes, clasped his hands in his lap, and a look of pathetic resignation crept over his long face. It is the way a country schoolmaster used to look in days long past when he had refused his school a holiday and it had risen against him in ill-mannered riot and violence and insurrection. Twice a motion to adjourn had been offered — a motion always in order in other Houses, and doubtless so in this one also. The President had refused to put these motions. By consequence, he was not in a pleasant place now, and was having a right hard time. Votes upon motions, whether carried or defeated, could make endless delay, and postpone the *Ausgleich* to next century.

In the midst of these sorrowful circumstances and this hurricane of yells and screams and satanic clatter of desk-boards, Representative Dr. Kronawetter un-feelingly reminds the Chair that a motion has been offered, and adds: "Say yes, or no! What do you sit there for, and give no answer?"

P. "After I have given a speaker the floor, I cannot give it to another. After Dr. Lecher is through, I will put your motion." [Storm of indignation from the Left.]

Wolf (to the Chair). "Thunder and lightning! look at the Rule governing the case!"

Kronawetter. "I move the close of the sitting! And I demand the ayes and noes!"

Dr. Lecher. "Mr. President, have I the floor?"

P. "You have the floor."

Wolf (to the Chair, in a stentorian voice which cleaves its way through the storm). "It is by such brutalities as these that you drive us to extremities! Are you waiting till some one shall throw into your face the word that shall describe what you are bringing about?* [Tempest of insulted fury from the Right.] *Is that what you are waiting for, old Grayhead?"* [Long-continued clatter of desk-boards from the Left, with shouts of "The vote! the vote!" An ironical shout from the Right, "Wolf is boss!"]

Wolf keeps on demanding the floor for his motion. At length —

P. "I call Representative Wolf to order! Your conduct is unheard-of, sir! You forget that you are in a parliament; you must remember where you are, sir." [Applause from the Right. Dr. Lecher is still

---

* That is, *revolution.*

the Ordner with a remark which Boss Tweed might
have translated into " Now let's see what you are
going to do about it!"   [Noise and tumult all over
the House.]

Wolf stands upon his rights, and says he will main-
tain them till he is killed in his tracks.   Then he re-
sumes his banging, the President jangles his bell
and begs for order, and the rest of the House aug-
ments the racket the best it can.

Wolf. " I require an adjournment, because I find
myself personally threatened. [Laughter from the
Right.]   Not that I fear for myself; I am only
anxious about what will happen to the man who
touches me."

The Ordner. " I am not going to fight with you."

Nothing came of the efforts of the angel of peace,
and he presently melted out of the scene and disappeared.   Wolf went on with his noise and with his
demands that he be granted the floor, resting his
board at intervals to discharge criticisms and epithets
at the Chair.   Once he reminded the Chairman of
his violated promise to grant him (Wolf) the floor,
and said, " Whence I came, we call promise-breakers
rascals!"   And he advised the Chairman to take his
conscience to bed with him and use it as a pillow.
Another time he said that the Chair was making itself
ridiculous before all Europe.   In fact, some of Wolf's
language was almost unparliamentary.   By-and-by he
struck the idea of beating out a *tune* with his board.
Later he decided to stop asking for the floor, and

to confer it upon himself.   And so he and Dr. Lecher now spoke at the same time, and mingled their speeches with the other noises, and nobody heard either of them.   Wolf rested himself now and then from speech-making by reading, in his clarion voice, from a pamphlet.

I will explain that Dr. Lecher was not making a twelve-hour speech for pastime, but for an important purpose.   It was the government's intention to push the *Ausgleich* through its preliminary stages in this one sitting (for which it was the Order of the Day), and then by vote refer it to a select committee. It was the Majority's scheme — as charged by the Opposition — to drown debate upon the bill by pure noise — drown it out and stop it.   The debate being thus ended, the vote upon the reference would follow — with victory for the government.   But into the government's calculations had not entered the possibility of a single-barreled speech which should occupy the entire time-limit of the sitting, and also get itself delivered in spite of all the noise.   Goliah was not expecting David.   But David was there; and during twelve hours he tranquilly pulled statistical, historical, and argumentative pebbles out of his scrip and slung them at the giant; and when he was done he was victor, and the day was saved.

In the English House an obstructionist has held the floor with Bible-readings and other outside matters; but Dr. Lecher could not have that restful and recuperative privilege — he must confine himself

15E

strictly to the subject before the House.   More than
once, when the President could not hear him because
of the general tumult, he sent persons to listen and
report as to whether the orator was speaking to the
subject or not.

The subject was a peculiarly difficult one, and it
would have troubled any other deputy to stick to it
three hours without exhausting his ammunition,
because it required a vast and intimate knowledge —
detailed and particularized knowledge — of the commercial, railroading, financial, and international bank-
ing relations existing between two great sovereignties,
Hungary and the Empire.   But Dr. Lecher is President of the Board of Trade of his city of Brünn, and
was master of the situation.   His speech was not
formally prepared.   He had a few notes jotted down
for his guidance; he had his facts in his head; his
heart was in his work; and for twelve hours he stood
there, undisturbed by the clamor around him, and
with grace and ease and confidence poured out the
riches of his mind, in closely reasoned arguments,
clothed in eloquent and faultless phrasing.

He is a young man of thirty-seven.   He is tall
and well-proportioned, and has cultivated and forti-
fied his muscle by mountain-climbing.   If he were a
little handsomer he would sufficiently reproduce for
me the Chauncey Depew of the great New England
dinner nights of some years ago; he has Depew's
charm of manner and graces of language and
delivery.

There was but one way for Dr. Lecher to hold the floor — he must stay on his legs. If he should sit down to rest a moment, the floor would be taken from him by the enemy in the Chair. When he had been talking three or four hours he himself proposed an adjournment, in order that he might get some rest from his wearing labors; but he limited his motion with the condition that if it was lost he should be allowed to continue his speech, and if it carried he should have the floor at the next sitting. Wolf was now appeased, and withdrew his own thousand-times offered motion, and Dr. Lecher's was voted upon — and lost. So he went on speaking.

By one o'clock in the morning, excitement and noise-making had tired out nearly everybody but the orator. Gradually the seats of the Right underwent depopulation; the occupants had slipped out to the refreshment-rooms to eat and drink, or to the corridors to chat. Some one remarked that there was no longer a quorum present, and moved a call of the House. The Chair (Vice-President Dr. Kramarz) refused to put it to vote. There was a small dispute over the legality of this ruling, but the Chair held its ground.

The Left remained on the battle-field to support their champion. He went steadily on with his speech; and always it was strong, virile, felicitous, and to the point. He was earning applause, and this enabled his party to turn that fact to account. Now and then they applauded him a couple of minutes on a stretch.

hope that the committee into whose hands this bill will eventually be committed will take its stand upon high ground, and will return the *Ausgleich-Provisorium* to this House in a form which shall make it the protector and promoter alike of the great interests involved and of the honor of our fatherland.'' After a pause, turning toward the government benches: '' But in any case, gentlemen of the Majority, make sure of this: henceforth, as before, you will find us at our post. The Germans of Austria will neither surrender nor die !''

Then burst a storm of applause which rose and fell, rose and fell, burst out again and again and again, explosion after explosion, hurricane after hurricane, with no apparent promise of ever coming to an end; and meantime the whole Left was surging and weltering about the champion, all bent upon wringing his hand and congratulating him and glorifying him.

Finally he got away, and went home and ate five loaves and twelve baskets of fishes, read the morning papers, slept three hours, took a short drive, then returned to the House and sat out the rest of the thirty-three-hour session.

To merely *stand up* in one spot twelve hours on a stretch is a feat which very few men could achieve; to add to the task the utterance of a hundred thousand words would be beyond the possibilities of the most of those few; to superimpose the requirement that the words should be put into the form of a compact, coherent, and symmetrical oration would probably rule out the rest of the few, bar Dr. Lecher.

III. CURIOUS PARLIAMENTARY ETIQUETTE

In consequence of Dr. Lecher's twelve-hour speech and the other obstructions furnished by the Minority, the famous thirty-three-hour sitting of the House accomplished nothing. The government side had made a supreme effort, assisting itself with all the helps at hand, both lawful and unlawful, yet had failed to get the *Ausgleich* into the hands of a committee. This was a severe defeat. The Right was mortified, the Left jubilant.

Parliament was adjourned for a week — to let the members cool off, perhaps — a sacrifice of precious time, for but two months remained in which to carry the all-important *Ausgleich* to a consummation.

If I have reported the behavior of the House intelligibly, the reader has been surprised at it, and has wondered whence these law-makers come and what they are made of; and he has probably supposed that the conduct exhibited at the Long Sitting was far out of the common, and due to special excitement and irritation. As to the make-up of the House, it is this: the deputies come from all the walks of life and from all the grades of society. There are princes, counts, barons, priests, peasants, mechanics, laborers, lawyers, judges, physicians, professors, merchants, bankers, shopkeepers. They are religious men, they are earnest, sincere, de-

o*⁎*⁎

voted, and they hate the Jews. The title of
Doctor is so common in the House that one may
almost say that the deputy who does not bear it is
by that reason conspicuous.   I am assured that it is
not a self-granted title, and not an honorary one, but
an *earned* one ; that in Austria it is very seldom conferred as a mere compliment ; that in Austria the
degrees of Doctor of Music, Doctor of Philosophy,
and so on, are not conferred by the seats of learning ;
and so, when an Austrian is called Doctor it means
that he is either a lawyer or a physician, and that
he is not a self-educated man, but is college-bred,
and has been diplomaed for merit.

That answers the question of the constitution of
the House.   Now as to the House's curious manners.
The manners exhibited by this convention of Doctors
were not at that time being tried as a wholly new experiment.   I will go back to a previous sitting in
order to show that the deputies had already had some
practice.

There had been an incident.   The dignity of the
House had been wounded by improprieties indulged
in in its presence by a couple of the members.   This
matter was placed in the hands of a committee to
determine where the guilt lay, and the degree of it,
and also to suggest the punishment.   The chairman
of the committee brought in his report.   By this it
appeared that, in the course of a speech, Deputy
Schrammel said that religion had no proper place
in the public schools — it was a private matter.